Smoke and Mirrors

The Magical World of
Chemical Dependency

Smoke and Mirrors

The Magical World of
Chemical Dependency

Dorothy Marie England

Foreword
Chilton R. Knudsen

Forward Movement
Cincinnati, Ohio

Dorothy Marie England is a pseudonym used in deference to Alocoholic Anonymous' (A.A.) tradition of anonymity at the level of the press. A recovering alcoholic and drug addict, Ms. England practiced as a Certified Addiction Counselor for many years and served as Director of Alcohol and Drug Programs for a regional mental health center. She wrote numerous articles and books that were published in national professional journals and by Forward Movement. Ms. England, a mother and grandmother, died in March 2008.

© 2021, 2019, 2016, 2012, 2007, 2004, 1995 Forward Movement

Cover Design: Albonetti Design

ISBN: 978-0-88028-166-9

www.forwardmovement.org

This book is dedicated to Rosalie, who gave me the idea of the evil magician; and to the Alcoholics Anonymous group in Georgia who brought me out of illusion and into reality.

Contents

Foreword

Imagine a terminal disease, progressive and fatal, that includes within its spectrum of symptoms a tenacious illusion: a powerful and resolute illusion that the patient is completely free of that very disease. From this symptom of denial, a number of false certainties are liberated. For example, some other cause is always to blame for the latest disruption in life—not the disease. The patient is certain that she is absolutely disease-free. In fact, he most likely possesses an inherent immunity to ever contracting that disease. Other people suffer this disease. Pity them. But not me.

The identified symptoms of this disease, even though they are manifestly present in the individual, must be due to some other condition. Perhaps it's a temporary condition, manageable through efforts to control the symptoms. Or it might be a situational condition; geographic relocation or entrance into a new relationship, job, or counseling will be the remedy. This disease, and its concurrent denial, stalks its victims relentlessly. As the disease progresses, the denial about the disease escalates.

Life circumstances might include symptoms similar to the identified symptoms of this terminal disease. But the denial/illusion persists. The patient is certain that the symptoms are misdiagnosed or stem from some other exotic disease, some psychological malady or odd allergy that awaits the proper diagnosis.

People with any progressive disease like Parkinson's Disease, arthritis, or heart disease often go through a stage of denial about their disease. But in most cases, that denial fades as symptoms progress. Most patients of these diseases acknowledge the reality of their illness and move into an acceptance of the appropriate treatment. This stage of acceptance enables them to move into treatment and enhance their quality of life. Not so with the disease of addiction.

What can we say about a disease whose spectrum of indicators includes denial as a primary symptom? How can we begin to get well if our disease tells us we are not sick? We could call this conundrum an instance of insanity—irrational and surreal. That would be accurate. We who know about addiction understand the solemn truth that addiction is primarily a disease of denial, illusion, and deception. We know that treatment and healing begin with a First Step: an acceptance that this is indeed the truth about our disease, no matter how the symptom of denial may try to mislead us.

We know, firsthand, that addiction is a disease that is cunning, baffling, and powerful. We know this disease is like a virus: it enslaves spirit, mind, and body to perpetuate its own existence. It is like cancer; it invades our being and multiplies within us, sucking into itself the very nutrients that enable life to continue. We know that addiction is cruel and unsparing and tenacious. Because denial is a key symptom, the beginning of recovery—which hinges on accepting the truth—is jeopardized.

The author of this book uses the Evil Magician as a metaphor for addiction. As the magician uses sleight-of-hand, illusion, and deception to confuse our perceptions, so too does addiction obscure the truth of its power and presence in the lives of many of us. The author always reminds us that the path to freedom and healing depends on truth and is sustained in truth. For people of every faith background or philosophical orientation, Truth is the foundation of life in its fullness. All healing begins with acceptance of truth and Truth.

May everyone who reads this book be convicted by its stark candor and inspired by the author's passion for spirituality. And may those who suffer from addiction in all its forms find in this book sufficient truth to make them uncomfortable and enough hope to help them take a step toward healing. The evil magician tells us a lie; the author tells us the truth.

Chilton R. Knudsen
IIIX Bishop of Maine

Smoke and Mirrors

The Magical World of Chemical Dependency

This book is for anyone interacting with a chemically dependent sufferer, whether family, friend, employer, or therapist. Chemical dependency is an illness which is primary, progressive, and terminal if allowed to follow its natural course. It is primary in that it is not the result of any outside cause nor is it a symptom of any other condition; it is not because of any of the reasons we who are chemically dependent put forward to explain or justify it. It is not because we were abused as children, although many of us were. It is not because our jobs are too stressful, although in many cases they are. It is not because no one loves or understands us, although frequently that is the case. Chemical dependency is biologically determined, just as is diabetes or heart disease.

Chemical dependency is progressive. One of the great mysteries of the disease, but one to which those in recovery attest, is that whether or not the sufferer uses chemicals or has addictive behaviors, the disease process progresses during periods of abstinence. If the drinker quits and resumes drinking ten years later, she finds that the disease has continued to progress. Very quickly she will be as ill as she would have been if she had been drinking all those years. If the gambler abstains for twenty years, the disease continues on its way, and should gambling resume, life will deteriorate as quickly as if there were never a hiatus.

Chemical dependency is also terminal. While many, especially those who suffer from behavioral addictions, succumb to accidents and secondary illnesses, the natural progression of the disease ends in death. We are all familiar with the life-threatening consequences of dependence on alcohol, nicotine, and cocaine, but the behavioral addictions take their toll as well. Stress dependency leads to cardiovascular disease, and a lowered immune system brought about by chronic stress leaves the sufferer less defended against cancer. Besides accidents and violence, sex addicts are threatened by sexually transmitted diseases. Gamblers suffer from stress-related illnesses as well as an increased risk of suicide.

Chemical dependency is a disease of the mind, body, and spirit. Deception is its primary spiritual symptom. Deception is an integral part of our human experience. Everyone dissembles to some degree. The philosopher Diogenes searched in vain for an honest man. But while most people lie a little, and some lie a little more, deception and illusion become vital to the maintenance of chemical dependency. Like cancer, this disease seems to have a life of its own, and this life struggles to survive. Paradoxically, also like cancer, if the life in the disease succeeds, the host organism and the disease both die. But struggle it does, until the host sufferer feels as though an evil civil war were raging inside. In this mystifying illness, the ultimate deception lies in fooling sufferers into believing they will die if they do not feed the disease that is killing them.

Those who are in relationship with the chemically dependent become trapped in the illness along with the sufferer. They also experience the progression of this disease of the feelings. Hopelessness, helplessness, anger, and frustration are common feelings of the chemically dependent and those who suffer with them, as are feelings of isolation and specialness. All of these feelings are the result of the illusions and delusions mastered by the chemically dependent, which are always comorbid with the disease. So adept are sufferers at deception, they may make it appear as if those with whom they are in relationship are the ones who are at fault.

Readers may see some traits of their own in the stories which follow. Remember, chemically dependent people are basically no different from others, but their disease greatly exaggerates their feelings and fears, and so their character defects are exaggerated. Like actors on a stage, their behavior is larger than life. Deception is always a spiritual problem. Feelings of confusion, helplessness, and hopelessness are symptoms of spiritual illness. Once we consider all the substances of abuse and add in the behavioral addictions, it is difficult to find anyone who is not touched by one manifestation of this disease or another. The spiritual sickness associated with chemical dependency may, in fact, be one of the primary spiritual problems plaguing humankind.

Yet all the news about chemical dependency is not bad; it is also a recoverable illness. With proper intervention, sufferers may regain their physical, mental, emotional, and spiritual health. In fact, magical as it may seem, many who recover do so with such vigor, freedom, and joy that they consider themselves fortunate for having had the disease. It is not unusual at a meeting of Alcoholics Anonymous or Narcotics Anonymous to hear recoverers identify themselves as grateful recovering alcoholics or addicts, meaning not only that they are grateful for their recovery, but they are also grateful that their disease brought them face to face with themselves and reality and led them to a place where they could discover spirituality. Information, understanding, communication, and communion with others already in recovery can dispel the illusions, bringing the chemically dependent and those who suffer with them into the real world. Getting well is a remarkable spiritual journey. This journey must be taken individually with the help and guidance of others who have made it. Paradoxically, we must do it ourselves but we cannot do it alone. Then, in recovery, we find that although nothing external may have changed, everything will be different.

To begin the journey, we first discover we have been traveling in the wrong direction. Chemical dependency is a disease of magical illusion—smoke and mirrors. It is a spiritual illness of lies and deception. In this disorder, both the sufferer and others in relationship are deluded. Come along and uncover the sorcerer's tricks in a performance where even the magician is fooled!

CHAPTER ONE

Another World

Alien, strange, as if they were from another world; these are the feelings of those who suffer from chemical dependency. Often these feelings begin in early childhood. The chemically dependent perceive themselves as different from others, isolated and misunderstood. And their feelings *are* different. Chemically dependent people suffer from disordered neurochemistry (brain chemistry) that alters their feelings and perceptions, causing them to feel lonely even with those they love and sad even when everything is fine. As they grow up, they create an environment that matches their feelings.

People expect and want their feelings to match their situation; they like the outside to match the inside. So, if they feel depressed but there is no external reason, they invent or create one. Because of their disordered neurochemistry, the chemically dependent seek out a negative environment or alter a positive one to fit their negative feelings. In early childhood they may have friends but will complain that no one likes them. As lovely, bright children, they will complain that they are dumb and ugly. Although they may have been football stars, cheerleaders, and prom queens, over time their self-fulfilling prophesies come to pass. Sufferers abuse their bodies and talents until they appear dull and ugly and people shun them. Eventually, true to their predictions, they become disliked and misunderstood. They become isolated and lonely, comfortable only with others who, like themselves, enjoy intoxication, chemical and adrenaline highs, and conflict. The chemically dependent use substances and behaviors to alter these distressing feelings and perceptions. They use chemicals and behaviors, attempting to feel normal.

The disordered brain chemistry sufferers experience is related to lowered levels of neurotransmitters: chemical messengers that affect mood, pain perception, impulse control, cognition, memory, sleep, hormones, body temperature, cardiovascular function, sexuality, appetite, and gastrointestinal function. These neurochemical dysfunctions may be genetically determined or a result of trauma. Chemically dependent people learn that certain chemicals and behaviors alter brain chemistry, creating feelings of well-being. All addictive behaviors and substances of abuse adjust neurotransmitter levels. All stimulate the activity of a neurotransmitter called serotonin. Low levels of serotonin produce feelings of depression, anxiety, irritability, anger, forgetfulness, an inability to concentrate, cravings, heightened pain perception, poor impulse control, and an inability to feel happy. If the condition is genetically predisposed, these feelings begin in very early childhood and continue until recovery or death. The chemicals and behaviors the chemically dependent discover to alter this faulty brain chemistry are often unacceptable to family and society, yet sufferers are driven by a compelling need to use the chemicals and enact the behaviors, believing they cannot survive without them. Use of the chemicals and behaviors is perceived as vital. And, like most people, sufferers will go to any length to survive.

The chemicals of abuse are familiar to most and include alcohol; cocaine; heroin; the hallucinogens such as LSD; cannabis; minor tranquilizers such as Valium, Xanax, and Ativan; sleeping pills; opioids for pain such as Oxycontin, Percodan, Tylenol III, and Vicodin; caffeine; nicotine; sugar; fat; salt; and complex carbohydrates. The behaviors of abuse include anything that produces an adrenaline rush or a steady state of adrenaline elevation, such as gambling, fighting (physical and psychological), risky or aberrant sexual behavior, dangerous activities such as racing, stealing, lying, games, and computer use, overspending, stressful exercise, and stressful work. Chemically dependent people feel they will die without the behavior and/or the chemicals. You've heard the expressions "dying for a drink," "dying for a cigarette," "dying for a date," "dying to go shopping." This isn't a hyperbole; sufferers feel driven to do and use to survive.

But society and the families, friends, and coworkers of the chemically dependent are often harmed because of the behaviors and see that the chemical or behavior is damaging the sufferer. People begin to complain; consequences are imposed. In an environment where those on whom the sufferers are dependent insist that the use and behavior stop, what can the chemically dependent do? How can they feed the disease?

Chemically dependent people live in another world. They live in a magical world where nothing is real. Nothing is as it seems. People involved with them are like observers/participants in a magic show. Everything about the chemically dependent person is an illusion—everything is a trick in order to get and do what they believe they must. Chemically dependent people think everyone who cares about them should engage in the deception that they feel guarantees their survival—no matter how they and others may be hurt by the use/behavior. Chemically dependent people believe the harm they cause is minimal compared to their own need for the chemical/behavior. As for society in general or family and acquaintances who do not "care" enough about them to help them continue to use and do the behaviors, they are not worth consideration. The chemically dependent are "me first" people due to their overwhelming addictive disorder that others do not experience and cannot understand. In other words, chemically dependent people are the most selfish people on earth—not by intent, but because of their perception of excessive and overpowering need. Fear is at the core of life in the chemically dependent: fear they will not get what they need or that what they have will be lost. Fear is the foundation of all spiritual sickness. Every selfish thought, every defensive act is fear based. Every lie, every deception is rooted in fear. And only a spiritual awakening, only faith, "only perfect love can cast out fear" (1 John 4:18).

Chemically dependent people who are not recovering *never* tell the truth. Experiencing a different world, they distort reality to protect themselves. Their lives *become* a deception. Living with a sufferer is like living with a magician who is always on stage. Life is full of surprises. Nothing is sure, nothing is stable;

20

reality shifts and changes. Magical addicts alter the world to suit their needs, and everyone around them is caught up in the show.

The chemically dependent are people you might not have recognized until now. If their act is good, and it usually is, you will not realize they are chemically dependent until you get information such as this book provides. Some are obese. They are people who binge on or abstain from food, who drink or use other drugs more than you feel is good for them, who blame others for their feelings, who are angry a lot but say they are good humored. They may spend more money than they should, take risks with money or health/life/relationships, engage in risky, illicit sex, overwork and have jobs/relationships which are stressful; they may steal, shoplift, fight, and murder. They physically/sexually and/or emotionally abuse their children, their parents, their spouse, their friends, their coworkers. They lie and, when you discover it, they tell you that you are mistaken, or crazy, or act angry because you do not trust them. Their lives are erratic, full of ups and downs. Everything is larger than life. Everything is exaggerated. They take everything personally. They take everything seriously. They thrive on excitement, even negative excitement, which seems easier to come by than positive excitement. In any relationship where you feel bewildered or abused, you may be in a relationship with one who is chemically dependent. In any relationship where you find yourself on an emotional roller coaster or dragged down to the pits of despair, it is a good bet that it is with someone who is chemically dependent.

We are charming, exciting, pitiful, powerful, and helpless. Watch out for us, because we are deadly. Our needs are so different from yours, we will hurt you and hardly notice doing it.

I am chemically dependent and so are some members of my family. It is in our best interest for others who are not chemically dependent to understand us. Help received from those who do not understand us is deadly; it is called enabling. And others need protection from us. Not only are we physically dangerous, but we also deplete physical resources as we devour spirits and souls.

Here are some glimpses of lives of the chemically dependent:

Jack is in management. He is trying to abstain from alcohol because he has been embarrassed by his drinking behavior many times. He attends a conference where alcohol is served and drinking is the norm. It is 7 p.m. He decides he will have just one drink to be sociable. At 3 a.m., Jack falls into his bed in his hotel. During the course of the evening, he has consumed twenty alcoholic drinks. He has told several important people what he thinks and made inappropriate sexual advances toward colleagues. Unasked and off-key, he sang with the pianist at the banquet. His wake-up call comes at 7 a.m. He feels physically ill and cannot remember anything that happened the previous evening after 8 p.m.

Jane is the wife of a surgeon and mother of three teenagers. She is the adult child of an alcoholic physician. She has "bad nerves" and has been taking prescribed Xanax. Prior to the Xanax she took Valium for several years. Actually, she has Xanax prescriptions from two doctors, neither of whom is aware of the other. She prides herself in not using alcohol. One of the major stresses in Jane's life is her poor memory. Frequently she forgets appointments. She forgets what she wants to buy at the store and forgets to pick up her children. She forgets if she has taken her medicine or not and frequently overtakes it. She cannot understand what is happening; she is afraid and depressed. She cries secretly and has angry outbursts with the family. She also has difficulty sleeping and thinks she should see a doctor for a prescription for sleeping pills.

Joey is a child of chemically dependent parents. Joey often has trouble in school and at home. He has been diagnosed with attention deficit hyperactivity disorder. Often Joey cannot sit still, feeling an overpowering urge to be active, to run and jump and climb, and to fight. He needs motion and excitement. He also craves sweets. Joey has trouble sleeping at night, is fearful, and frequently has nightmares. His pediatrician is considering medication.

When Frank was a little boy, an older boy showed him some pornography. Frank was fascinated. When he got home, he masturbated for the first time. Now he has a collection of pornography. The pornography he searches out has grown progressively more graphic, perverse, and violent. Frank tries to have sexual relations with women, and he has even convinced some to try the bizarre things he sees in his materials. But this is never really satisfying. He wonders if anything will ever satisfy him other than masturbation accompanied by pornographic fantasies.

Ethel loves bingo. She plays it three times a week and says with a laugh that it is her only vice. Ethel's husband is a mechanic and has a good income, yet they always seem to be in debt. The family goes without new clothes and there is little money for life's little extras. Ethel thinks she wins at bingo. Both Ethel and her husband would be quite surprised to learn she consistently loses close to $50 per week.

Peter has always been concerned about his weight. As a child he was teased by other children because he was heavy, and his weight impaired his ability to play sports. He was always the last one chosen for the team. As an adult, Peter has tried numerous diets. They almost all worked, but after each diet he gained back more weight than he had lost. Now he is on a physician-supervised liquid diet and has had wonderful success and feels great. But he is almost consumed with fear because soon he will have to begin eating again, and he knows that he will gain back all the weight he lost and more.

For Sue and Jimmy, every night is fight night. Tensions begin to rise each afternoon just before they come home from work. Sue knows something will make Jimmy mad. Jimmy knows Sue will have done something wrong, demonstrating she does not love him as she should. The children anticipate the knots that will be in their stomachs, making them unable to eat supper as they cringe from the angry words and possible blows. They dread being picked up and wish they could live at daycare forever.

Sam is a minister who likes crisis counseling. He is a competent preacher, but his real love is helping those who are experiencing serious problems. He makes himself available to those he counsels as much as possible. He frequently gets calls in the night. Often his family activities or days off are interrupted by an emergency from one of his counselees.

Doris is having a stressful day at work. This is not unusual. She has difficulty accepting others' mistakes and limitations and is frequently in conflict with peers and supervisors. She often says, "Anything worth doing should be done well," and believes others should uphold this principle. Doris has little patience with laziness or error. She will work overtime this evening to clear up messes left by others. Then she will go home exhausted and dream about work.

George is overwhelmed by the amount of things he and his family need. He is almost always involved in making purchases or planning to make purchases. He is worried about the family finances. The checking account is frequently overdrawn and all the charge accounts are over the limit. He sincerely tries to restrict his purchases, but there is always some unfulfilled need that seems vital to family functioning.

Come along with these and other magicians on a journey through the magical world of chemical dependency. At times on the journey we may feel like one reading the sign at the entrance to Dante's hell: "All hope abandon, ye who enter here." Chemical dependency's prime illusion is that of hopelessness. But spiritual death can lead to resurrection; in utter powerlessness we encounter a loving power greater than ourselves.

CHAPTER TWO

The Shell Game

In the Shell Game, you are asked to identify the shell under which the bean lies. The magician appears to place a bean under one of three shells, then quickly shifts the position of the shells while you try to follow the moves. You guess which shell covers the bean when they come to rest, and, of course, you guess wrong. In reality, the magician never placed the bean under any shell. You cannot find it because it is not there.

Peter is a surgeon. He often regrets his choice of specialty, believing his weight problem is related to his stressful work. Not only is doing surgery stressful, he is often called out for emergencies and must work through regular meal times, which he believes contributes to his eating disorder. Peter frequently complains to his family about the stress and irregularity of his work as well as the stupidity, incompetence, and lack of ethical concern among his coworkers and other hospital staff. His family members do what they can to make his life pleasant and consistent while trying to get their own needs met. But their efforts to please are often unsuccessful, and he frequently says they are inconsiderate and unconcerned, selfish and unfeeling. He believes they don't appreciate all the things he does for them.

In chemical dependency, blame is the bean. The chemically dependent person will appear to place the bean (blame) under your shell, then shift everything around so that you also believe the bean (blame) is under the job's shell, or the children's shell. Everyone close to the sufferer tries to locate the blame, find the bean, but it always shifts and changes. When the magician pauses the game momentarily so you can guess, you inevitably guess wrong and the game begins again.

You believe the blame may be yours because you have done or failed to do something. You confess your fault, promising to change your behavior. The magician then says you are wrong, that the blame is really the boss's. If you talk to the boss and an agreement is made to change something stressful about the job, the blame will then be the children's. If you change the behavior of the children, the blame will be yours again. If you could change everything in the present to meet the needs of the chemically dependent, then the blame would move to the past: bad or inadequate parents, an unhappy childhood, etc.

Consider the following scene: The father is asked by his child to attend a ball game in which the child is a player. The chemically dependent father refuses to attend, saying it will interfere with his work schedule; in reality it will interfere with his drinking. The child's feelings are hurt and he storms off, saying the father does not care about him. The mother points out that the child is hurt. The father argues that the child should not have such a selfish attitude, that it is the rap music the mother allows him to buy that causes him to be so disrespectful. The father then says that he hates that his job has unreasonable requirements which render him incapable of being a good father, but he must keep this job so the mother and child may spend exorbitant amounts of money.

The chemically dependent person will go to any lengths to place blame or create blame where none exists—and will be so convinced of it that eventually you may also become convinced, even though rationally you know it is not true! Like magicians, chemically dependent persons are very skilled at deception, causing you to believe even though your mind knows what you see is an illusion. Needing to drink, smoke, take pills, abuse sugar, fat, and carbohydrates, or abuse adrenaline through arguing because of a lazy spouse, stressful job, or ungrateful children makes no sense. Logically, when a person has problems the problems need to be addressed. Rationally, using noxious chemicals which cause confusion, depression, sleeplessness, anxiety, irrational elation, obesity, illness, hangovers, cardiovascular disease, and dangerous, deviant behavior is a most doubtful solution to any problem. Yet a chemically dependent person can make this strange behavior appear to be the only reasonable answer.

Everyone has problems. Everyone suffers. Everyone has triumphs. Everyone has joys. For most people, these situations and feelings are things to be experienced, comprehended, and shared. For the chemically dependent, every experience or feeling is a reason to use chemicals. The basis of the disease is a disordered brain chemistry. Therefore, any and every thing that happens may be translated into an event calling for use of chemicals or of behavior that alters neurochemistry. For most of us, an event is an end in itself. For the chemically dependent, the event is never an end in itself, but points toward the need to and becomes a reason to use chemicals, either those we ingest or those we release in our brains by our thoughts and behavior. This is why, callous as it seems, chemically dependent people may use the death of someone they *love* as an excuse to use chemicals, argue, or do destructive behavior. They can use their wedding as a reason to become hopelessly drunk and blackout, not remembering their honeymoon night. For most people, life itself is the goal; for the chemically dependent person, getting and using the chemical or doing the neurochemical-changing behavior is the goal. The term "love" above is in italics because chemically dependent sufferers lose much more than life, health, or wealth. Due to their illness they never develop a mature capacity to love. Love comes when a person has more goodness in life than they need, something more which spills over as love for another. The unrecovering chemically dependent always feel needy. This need always results in the pathological use of chemicals or behavior, causing their consuming, continuing need to direct blame away from themselves, and their inability to consider the needs and wants of others.

Of course, the blame is not real any more than the bean is under the shell. Chemical dependency is a disease that is no one's "fault," not even the sufferer's. Feeling blame is as much a mistake as expecting to find the bean under the shell. But the magic trick is just for fun; accepting blame in chemical dependency is toxic. Those who engage in the game suffer real, deep loss of self-respect, peace, and the ability to think rationally. As Al-Anon, the program for friends and families of alcoholics says, a relationship with a chemically dependent person makes one's life unmanageable and insane, and consumes one's energy to the point that others are excluded, so that children, other family, and friends suffer as well.

Blame's assumption is that you could do better if you tried. If you really loved me you would help me, if you really cared about me you would leave me alone. While insight that produces conviction of wrongdoing where wrongdoing exists can be a spiritual virtue, chronic guilt leads to spiritual illness. Conviction of wrongdoing says, "I'm sorry; with God's help I will not do that again." Guilt says, "I should have done better, I should have known better, I should have been better." Conviction says, "I made a mistake." Guilt says, "I am no good, I am worthless." Once the illusion of blame is accepted, guilt sets in. Then only a powerful spiritual intervention can interrupt the process. In the shell game, one concentrates so completely on the illusion that everything and everyone else is forgotten. In a sense, even the magician is forgotten and disappears, which brings us to chapter three.

The Disappearing Act

Chemically dependent people become expert at this form of magic. Their skills improve over time as their illness progresses, so that finally, as with every good magician, you come to expect that they will not be where they should be; they will pop up somewhere else.

Chemically dependent people become unable to keep commitments. They handle this in two ways. The first is by physically disappearing. They become too sick either to go or stay where they belong, and go somewhere else so they may hide, rest, or use chemicals to alter their neurochemistry. They may still be under the influence from last night and not want others to recognize it, so they hide. They may be so hungover that they cannot function and go somewhere to rest. Or they may have withdrawal symptoms or cravings so bad that they must use some stabilizing chemicals/behaviors, and so they disappear.

The second way they attempt to manage their disease by disappearing is through denial, a kind of psychological disappearance which is performed through a smoke and mirrors effect. Using denial, the chemically dependent person convinces you to see what is not there—and to not see what is. Using denial, these magicians cause you to believe they are not under the influence of chemicals, do not use chemicals/behaviors too much, that chemicals/behaviors are not the problem, and that you and other people, places, and things are. In other words, they disappear into a cloud of confusion, while you look into the mirror of projections, placing blame on yourself and/or others. Although the chemically dependent remain just where they were, you can no longer see them or the problem. After the show, you wonder how they did it.

Jack, feeling ill when the wake-up call comes, lies in bed and drifts back to sleep. When the effect of the alcohol wears off around 9 a.m., he gets up. He is too sick to move very fast. He drives the hundred miles home, suffering severe alcohol craving. When he arrives home, his wife expresses concern over his lateness. She worried that he may have had an accident. Jack bursts into an angry attack. He says she is not worried about him, that her concern is for herself because she is so dependent on his income. He says she is unable to live without him and that she should do something to improve herself and her ability to make money. He asks why she cannot fix herself up and be more attractive. He says that he was away working under great pressure while she lolled around the house doing nothing. This, he says, is apparent from the appearance of the house. He demands to know what she did with her time while he slaved away at the convention. As she tries to defend herself and her actions, he storms out of the house. While he is away, an associate calls to see if he is all right. His wife tells the associate he has gone out on business and everything is fine. Jack comes in about 3 a.m. heavily intoxicated. He has skillfully demonstrated both methods of orchestrating the disappearing act.

It is hard to tell which is the worst method of disappearance. Both are effective and both hurt. Is it worse to have an employee not show up for a meeting or to show up under the influence, focusing on personal problems to deflect attention from her condition and unable to carry out decisions made because she cannot remember them? Would you prefer to have Dad not show up for the children's birthday party or to show up intoxicated, taking over the party with complaints about his terrible day and about your inconsiderately arranging the party just at a time when it would interfere with his more important duties? Is it worse to have your child missing at Christmas or there, under the influence of adrenaline produced by anger, arguing violently about how awful you and everyone else in his life treat him? Does it hurt more for your spouse to miss dinner because of an illicit liaison or to be home, critical of your appearance, the house, and the meal?

For example, your wife is home fixing dinner. Unknown to you, she feels as though she may break in pieces—explode—because of conflicting and powerful needs. She needs to fix dinner and appear to be a "good wife," but she also needs to be with her lover. She is obviously uncomfortable, but when you ask what is wrong, she tells you she hates having to cook meals; that she works all day, then has to come home and slave over a

33

stove for you. You respond that she gets home earlier than you, and you will help with the dishes. She flies into a rage, saying your income is inadequate because you are so inept. She says that if you really cared about her, you would try harder to get a better job, or at least a raise so she could quit work. Railing about your deficits, she storms out of the house, feeling justified in fleeing to her lover. Your wife, like Jack, has skillfully pulled off both forms of the disappearing act. She first disappeared in a smoke-cloud of blame, leaving you staring in the mirror at your own unworthiness, then she physically disappeared to satisfy her compelling needs.

In the above situations, the chemically dependent person disappeared in a barrage of defenses, misdirecting attention away from his/her diseased condition to other people, places, and things. The magician usually implies that you could fix everything, that you have power over these people, places, and things and could make them perfect if only you would do it. Also either stated or implied is the accusation that you do not make everything right because you do not care. The magician directs your attention toward yourself, others, and the environment, making everything that is wrong your fault. While you stare into the mirror of your inadequacies, he/she disappears in a smoke screen of blame. Although physically present with all eyes focused on her/him, the sufferer disappears, leaving you alone with your guilty reflection, your unmet needs, and your angry, desperate feelings.

Psychologically, everyone likes to be in control. The desire for control is what prevents people from entering twelve-step programs, causing them to suffer so long. Attempts to control those who cannot control themselves are doomed to failure; they result in fear and anger. Anger is a powerful emotion that produces addictive adrenaline. While control is psychologically appealing to those who are in relationship with the chemically dependent, there is a danger in attempting to maintain such control. Anyone genetically predisposed to addictive disease may become dependent on the adrenaline produced through the inherent fear and excitement involved in such attempts. Just as you may enjoy a roller coaster ride, a magic show, juicy gossip, or a good mystery, you may be attracted to the challenge and excitement of attempting to control the chemically dependent by helping them. Once involved in such a relationship and finding them beyond control, you may feel miserable and complain bitterly, as you should. Yet, if finally freed of that sufferer, you may immediately become involved with another with the same illness. Unknowingly, you are again bedazzled by the act, not seeing the real person. The chemically dependent require someone to validate their excessive needs and assist in getting them met. Once more you are trapped by your own altruistic tendencies, along with your growing need to try to control the uncontrollable.

Chemically dependent people believe they are special people and, in a sense, they are. Each one believes no one has been like him/her since the beginning of time. Each feels isolated and alone, with special abilities, feelings, thoughts, and needs which no one can or will acknowledge or satisfy. To those in relationship with the chemically dependent, this is very romantic and attractive. What could be more special than the ability to make someone so uniquely unhappy happy? And the magician lures you deeper and deeper into the deception, telling you that you are the only one who can, that you are the only one who understands. But the happiness is short-lived, and you discover once again you were deceived; again you become the victim of the disappearing act.

In reality, the spiritual hole experienced by the chemically dependent cannot be filled by any human power. As Carl Jung discovered, this emptiness that all people experience but which is exacerbated in the chemically dependent can only be filled by a loving God.

CHAPTER FOUR

The Magic Hat

The magic hat is a favorite prop. The magician puts something into the hat, perhaps a scarf or gloves, then pulls out something entirely different, like a rabbit or a bird. The chemically dependent person is a magic hat, out of which come personality changes so profound that he/she can seem to be several different people in the space of just a few minutes. Those in relationship with a sufferer cannot predict which personality will appear at any time. The chemically dependent's personality may change before one's eyes, just as easily as the scarf changes into a bird.

Two emerging and opposing personalities of the chemically dependent are their apparently selfless and selfish selves. Sufferers may, on the one hand, seem completely altruistic, giving both resources and time to others who seemingly may not deserve their attention. On the other hand, they may disregard the feelings and needs of people close to them, behaving totally selfishly. These conflicting facets of personality confuse those with whom they are in relationship. Their ability to be thoughtfully selfless at times, childishly selfish at others, and especially their ability to be openly giving to people who should not be so important to them while they are thoughtless of those who should matter the most is mystifying.

For instance, Jane is on many committees in her church and community. She chairs several and holds office in others. Demonstrating great social responsibility, she is concerned about city beautification, the fine arts, the needy, the mentally ill, and the homeless. Sometimes Jane believes she is the only one truly committed to these issues. Others help, but in a casual, superficial, and often incompetent way. Jane feels her children are old enough to care for themselves and help out at home. She resents their demands on her time, believing they are selfish. She wishes she could instill in them some of her own selfless concern for others. Also, she feels her husband is selfish. As a physician, he is almost always working, supposedly helping others, but when he has time off and this conflicts with her duties and meetings, he thinks she should drop everything to be with him. She thinks the family does not take her work seriously, and their lack of appreciation is just one of the things that causes her to need minor tranquilizers. Her husband and children feel guilty and angry.

Two more opposing facets of personality that the chemically dependent demonstrate are relentless honesty and shameless dissemblance. They can go for the throat with amazing accuracy, uncovering others' faults and even their own when it is convenient. They appear honest, but when it suits their purposes, they blatantly lie about even small things. People are expected to be basically honest or dishonest. This chameleon-like ability to be either, depending on the situation, is confusing and unnerving.

Doris, pursuing her addiction to work, is an example. Occasionally, she makes a mistake. This, she feels, is because she has to take up slack for other employees who cannot or will not do their jobs properly. But Doris hates to make mistakes so much she often denies to herself and others that she makes them. When confronted with an error of judgment, she often lies. She is so defensive about her deficiencies that others usually will not risk engaging her anger by pointing them out. Occasionally, Doris will make a mistake so blatant she cannot hide or deny it. Or sometimes she will make such a tiny mistake she does not mind admitting it. Then she will come forward in a burst of engaging honesty and admit her fault. Inside, Doris feels others make mistakes much more often than she does, and that others' mistakes are due to moral lassitude or stupidity while her own are due to oversight because she has to carry others' loads. It is for these reasons that Doris feels compelled to point out others' errors while overlooking or denying her own. She sees herself as a moral force in the office; she must maintain an aura of perfection as an example for others who do not take things as seriously as they should. Unknowingly, Doris is addicted to endogenous chemicals she produces through stress, worry, and fear surrounding her need to appear perfect and stay in control.

The disease of chemical dependency keeps life's focus on getting and using the chemicals and doing the mood-changing behaviors, so honesty/dishonesty and altruism/selfishness become tools to meet biochemical needs rather than ends in themselves. Practicing alcoholics are not honest/dishonest in order to facilitate good/bad relationships, but in order to get and use alcohol. Gamblers are not altruistic/selfish because of concern or lack of it for others, but in order to continue their adrenaline-producing behavior. In the disease of chemical dependency, nothing is personal because the objective of all behavior is the alteration of brain chemistry. Relationships are secondary; neurochemical needs are primary. Saying to the sufferer, "If you loved me, you wouldn't drink, gamble, lie, eat so much, be selfish, run around, hit me, etc.," is like saying to someone, "If you loved me, you would stop breathing, or you would breathe only half as much." Sufferers see their dependencies as life sustaining; their behavior has nothing to do with relationships. Chemically dependent people will be honest or selfless if it doesn't interfere with using the chemicals or doing the behavior. Relationships may appear to come first so long as they do not interfere with the sufferer's need. Often the sufferer may tell a factual truth, but still lie; the facts are given not for the sake of honesty but in order to misdirect the enabler. Using the addictive chemicals or doing the addictive behavior is perceived as absolutely necessary to sustain the sufferer's life and *always* comes first.

Two other conflicting personality changes are elation and depression. Before your eyes, the chemically dependent person's mood may change from deep depression with suicidal thoughts to joyful optimism and playful fun. One minute everything seems hopeless, then magically these feelings are transformed. You may listen sympathetically and seemingly endlessly to the chemically dependent's sad tale, then be amazed when he/she gets a call with an invitation to come where addictive chemicals or behaviors are available and suddenly everything's fine. The person happily leaves you alone and depressed. It is not necessarily a party that does the magic. It may be business, a friend in need, or an ex-wife in trouble, but be assured the new activity involves a chemical or a behavior that will alter the chemically dependent's feelings toward the comfort level. Just anticipating such an activity has a powerful mood-changing effect.

Frank decides a stable family life may heal his need for pornography. He marries a lovely girl, goes to church, and they have children. He becomes active in the church, believing that if he is a "good" person, he will find the satisfaction he yearns for. Left to change his child's diapers, he remembers some of his renounced pedophilic pornography and begins to fantasize about touching her genitals. As time goes on, the fantasies become obsession. Eventually, Frank is sexually abusing his children and swearing them to secrecy. He is also watching pornographic videos on the Internet and showing them to the children. Frank continues to go to church and becomes a deacon. He leads Bible reading at home in the evenings. Frank is filled with self-loathing. The more he hates himself, the more rigid he is in his attempts to be "good." He becomes a religious zealot who is sure that he and his entire family are going to hell.

Frank demonstrates another conflicting personality change, of fluctuating between moralism and depravity. In an extreme manifestation of sex addiction, a chemically dependent sufferer may preach from the Bible, then molest children. The sufferer may work long hours to support the family he/she claims to love while physically and emotionally abusing them. The chemically dependent person may loudly complain about others' lies and dishonesty, yet be involved in extramarital affairs and chemical abuse. A sufferer who is obese from overeating sugar, fats, and carbohydrates may deride a relative who abuses alcohol or drugs. Both facets of personality appear real and true, leaving those in relationship feeling confused or even "crazy." How can someone preach morality one minute then abuse the family? How can someone espouse high moral values while engaging in sexual deviancy and chemical abuse? The chemically dependent do it with such skill that it appears effortless and natural.

Chemically dependent people may also go from fiscal conservative to lavish spender at the drop of a hat. They may watch every penny, bitterly complaining that the family is wasteful and spending too much money, while they, themselves, gamble, or lose or spend great sums of money while intoxicated, or buy drugs or sex. You may be told there is not enough money for Johnny's new school shoes while the paycheck is spent on alcohol before it arrives home. Money may not be found for the children to go to a movie, but mom or dad eat many dollars worth of snacks. There isn't enough money for home improvements yet gambling debts rise. You may be told you are spending too much on groceries while prostitutes are being paid or friends lavishly entertained. There may not be funds for therapeutic counseling or treatment while valuables are sold to buy cocaine.

If the relationship lasts long enough, these conflicting personality changes will begin to appear normal, eventually leaving you feeling at fault if you are not able to accept them. If you live with the magician and see the trick practiced daily, you begin to expect gloves to change into rabbits and scarves to turn into birds! Remember, in chemical dependency nothing is as it seems, nothing is true, nothing is permanent. The magician amazes and surprises so the unexpected is the only thing to expect. In a magic show that only lasts an hour, this is fun. But a lifetime of experiencing the unexpected produces confusion, and confusion produces fear. Living with fear over time can lead to addiction to the adrenaline it releases.

And living in this amorphous magical world where nothing is permanent and nothing is stable can lead one to believe everything is relative, that there are no everlasting truths, nothing immutable in which to trust. Living inside the sorcerer's illusion creates spiritual sickness in the unarmed. Coming into reality requires putting on the armor of a loving, powerful God.

CHAPTER FIVE

Card Tricks

Most magicians are adept at card tricks. They are relatively easy, take little equipment, and they are baffling. The magician shuffles some cards, has you pick one, then tells you which one you picked. You are amazed. Can he read your mind? How did she do it?

One way the magician knows which card you picked is because he manipulated the deck. Jimmy knows Sue hates to go out with him; it often ends in his demeaning and embarrassing her. Jimmy, on the other hand, enjoys being in public with Sue. It gives him the opportunity to appear to others as a solicitous husband whose efforts are often unappreciated. Anticipating her reluctance, he calls her mom and suggests she invite them over for supper and a card game on Friday night. By the way, he says, do not tell Sue he called; she will really like it that her mom is thinking of her. Coming home, he appears to be in a good mood, and asks Sue what she would like to do this weekend. Surprised and relieved at his good humor, she says she would like to stay home, maybe they can rent a movie and watch it after the kids go to bed. He smiles and says that sounds great. Later her mom calls and offers the invitation. She asks Jimmy what he wants to do. He says he would just as soon stay home, as she suggested. Although she fears his reaction, she bravely says she really does not want to hurt her mom's feelings. Cheerfully, Jimmy tells her it is up to her; if she wants to go to her mom's, that is what they will do. Of course, Friday night ends in tears for both Sue and her mom. Jimmy tells her it is all her fault for choosing to go to her mom's instead of staying home with him and watching a movie. Like the participant in a card trick, Sue knows she has been manipulated but cannot imagine how it was done.

Ethel played bingo last Friday and lost more than usual. The number of cards she plays has been increasing, and Friday, she lost on them all. It was a bad time of the month to sustain such a loss. Saturday morning Ethel has to face the fact that there is not enough food money to last through the end of the month. She is terrified this loss will show her gambling as a problem, and her husband will put a stop to it. Although she knows from comments her husband has made that he secretly wishes she would get a job, she has resisted going to work in the past because she honestly believed mothers should stay home to raise the children. On this Saturday morning, she remembers a friend who asked if she were interested in a job. She calls the friend, gets the job, and fixes her husband a surprise dinner during which she tells him the wonderful news. She rationalizes away her guilt over leaving the children alone in the afternoons; after all, in every family she knows both parents have to work to make ends meet in today's economy. She wonders why she resisted working for so long. Ethel has accurately guessed and played the card her husband would choose, the one which will make him happy, and which will deflect his attention from the cause of their financial problems.

The chemically dependent person always seems to know which card you are holding. Just when you are the angriest, the sufferer does what will make you forgive her, even before your anger is expressed. Just when you are the most hopeless, the chemically dependent will change his behavior to give you hope. The sufferer always seems to know which card you are choosing. If you have planned to leave, he anticipates this and makes a move that convinces you that you should not. If you have decided to throw her out, she seems to know what is on your mind and convinces you that she needs you and will change. If you have made an appointment to get help for yourself, he tells you you do not need help, that he is the one at fault. If you have arranged for an intervention or legal commitment for her treatment, she appears sober and radiantly healthy, causing you to wonder why you believed things were so bad.

Chemically dependent people are facile at guessing your secret guilt card. They identify with stunning accuracy just the thing about which you feel most guilty and exploit it. If a mother, you may have neglected the children or house because you had to work to supplement the family income. You may be denying your guilt over this even to yourself. But the sufferer identifies your guilty feelings like the magician identifies the card you hid in the deck. You may have done everything possible to cover up an indiscretion, but the chemically dependent seems to know intuitively what you have done and expose and exploit it. This talent for uncovering others' faults is amazing. Yet sufferers do not identify your faults because they are hurt, although they may express deep hurt with great conviction. As with the rest of their behavior, they go to the heart of your guilt in order to take attention away from themselves. This is one of the ways they effect the psychological disappearing act we mentioned before. Once they identify your guilt, they disappear, leaving you distracted and consumed with self-defense.

The chemically dependent also know your "wish card." This is the card that holds your fondest dreams of fun and relationship. Really, you have communicated these wishes many times, but you were sure the sufferer was not paying attention. Then, just when you have reached the end of your rope, he presents you with just what you were wishing for. This can be as simple as bringing or sending flowers, making a date for dinner or the movies, or inviting friends over. It can also be as important as asking your mother or grandchildren to visit or going to church with you. Since you are unaware you have communicated your wishes, you are surprised, flattered, and pleased that the sufferer guessed just what you would like, believing this may signal an important change for the better. But you are fooled twice; first by not seeing how your wish was communicated, second by believing the chemically dependent person is doing something for you because he values your relationship. The relationship is always secondary at best. With the chemically dependent, the primary reason for any relationship is to gain help/permission (enabling) to continue to use the chemical or do the mood-changing behavior.

In the long years of clinical practice with chemically dependent people, I have frequently seen them wiggle out of what seemed to be inevitable entry into treatment through appearing to abstain or reduce the use of chemicals. Often this was accomplished even though the sufferer had no conscious awareness that others had made the decision to enter them into treatment. Fortunately for them, this appearance of health and changed behavior usually is short-lived, so those in relationship may soon get on with their plans for treatment. How sufferers know to change their behavior is a mystery. Perhaps the family, friends, or employer drops clues that are picked up unconsciously by the object of the treatment intervention. At any rate, frequently they do seem to sense danger and manage to convince others for a short time that they are O.K. They know you are holding a "treatment card" and alter their behavior accordingly.

You may be awestruck by the chemically dependent magician's god-like powers. But whenever you experience awe, you automatically perceive yourself to be less than the object of awe. Living or working over time in a situation where you feel less than someone else lowers your self-esteem. Living with a magician whose tricks you cannot understand or anticipate invites you to feel powerless and worthless. If continued long enough, you may even become dependent on the chemically dependent to define who you are, and you may lose even more self-esteem because of your inability to make this powerful person happy.

Many people are born into chemically dependent families, families where no matter what you do, authority figures often scream, "Off with your head. I know which choice you made and it is wrong!" Having always lived in a magical wonderland, such people have never been on the reality side of the looking glass. In order to discover the truth, the enabler may need an intervention in the form of a powerful spiritual experience. Issues of self-esteem are spiritual issues. When I compare myself to others, I always come out either better or worse. If better, I feel more worthy, and cannot experience a direct, level relationship. If worse, I feel I am less than worthy and cannot have a horizontal relationship. Only by basing my self-esteem on my higher power's evaluation of me, the same loving God who created us all, can I relate to others in a spirit of equality and assertiveness.

CHAPTER SIX

The Escape Act

The magician is bound with ropes or chains, which are usually made fast by a volunteer from the audience who ties the knots or secures the locks. The magician is then enclosed in some kind of box or bag and perhaps submerged in water or hung from a height, so that escape appears impossible. The audience holds its collective breath, then suddenly the magician appears, free and smiling.

While I was working as a counselor for the U.S. Army's alcohol and drug program, a staff sergeant was brought in deeply under the influence of alcohol and escorted by military police and his commander. He was a highly competent soldier who suffered from chemical dependency. The disease had progressed so far that those he worked with could no longer avoid bringing him in for treatment. The man was angry and combative, obviously in need of detoxification and residential care. His immediate admission to the hospital was arranged, and his commander accompanied him through the admission process. The next day, the sergeant simply walked off the hospital floor. He escaped! Several days later he was found intoxicated and again placed in the hospital. No one expected a seasoned soldier with such an impeccable record to leave the hospital after being placed there by his commanding officer. It seemed impossible. In fact, it took a while for the hospital staff and his military associates to believe it.

More recently, a woman was convicted of a drug-related crime in a county court and fined. Told the fine might be reduced or even revoked if she would submit to residential treatment for cocaine dependency, the woman agreed. Accepted for treatment, she was placed on a waiting list. When a bed became available in a few days, the woman told the treatment facility she had changed her mind and did not need to come. In the meantime, her fine had been revoked. She, too, escaped!

More often, the chemically dependent person's escapes are not quite so obvious, but are just as real. Typically, the sufferer escapes from your influence or your plans for them, rather than physically leaving the scene.

For instance, your child may be chronically and dangerously overweight, so you decide to limit his sugar. You make sure there are no sweets in the house and that he will not get money to buy them. Yet he escapes your control and continues to gain weight. He is getting sweets at several friends' homes, telling them his mom is on a diet, so he cannot get sweets at home.

Or, the act may take this form. Your husband suffers from sex addiction. You insist that he make a promise not to use pornography. Not only does he agree, he also finds a new interest—working out at the gym several times a week. Eventually you discover through a mutual friend that as well as having pornography in his locker, instead of always going to the gym, at least once a week he goes to an X-rated theater nearby.

The need to use the chemicals or to do the addictive behavior is so compelling that even the strongest bonds are unable to prevent sufferers from doing what they perceive as necessary to alter their neurochemistry. The emotional bonds of marriage, the parent/child relationship—no relationship is powerful enough to alter the course of addiction. Often, even the threat of death itself will not intervene in the disease process. Doctors tell of cancer patients continuing to smoke cigarettes after extensive lung, mouth, or throat surgery, of diabetics who continue to abuse sugar, of those addicted to sex continuing their pursuits in spite of the threat of HIV/AIDS, and of those who suffer from cardiovascular disease continuing their angry, stressful lifestyles.

Doris's case illustrates this. She has developed a serious cardiovascular condition. The doctor gave her medication and told her to alter her eating habits and her lifestyle. He made it clear that stress is a major contributor to her condition, and that if she does not relax the result may be fatal. The doctor's admonitions make Doris angry. He must know she has to work for a living. She has had this job for years, and certainly cannot quit at her age and find a new position. Besides, if she were to leave there is no telling what would happen at the agency. She feels the doctor is unrealistic and is, himself, exaggerating her condition. She thinks perhaps she should find another, more sympathetic doctor. However, she decides it will be worthwhile to tell her employer and coworkers about her condition. This information may make them less quick to abuse her. Doris tells everyone at home and at work about her delicate heart. Now people walk on eggs around her even more. Doris has effectively escaped from any feedback about her behavior.

Spouses, family, employers, and friends may elicit promises, make threats, and deliver ultimatums, going to any length to impose controls on the chemically dependent's behavior. All of these will ultimately fail. The chemically dependent will wiggle out of promises and break any bonds. Threats and ultimatums will go unnoticed, since the sufferer does not believe in consequences. Disbelief in consequences is an integral psychological component of this physiological disorder. Even when faced with consequences, the chemically dependent does not believe them. He never believes you will fire him. She never believes you will leave her. This irrationality persists even after you have fired him or left her. The chemically dependent will continue to pursue the spouse or employer as though nothing has happened until he develops another enabling, codependent relationship. The only way to control behavior is to impose consequences. Since the chemically dependent simply will not believe in the existence of consequences, even in the face of them, controls never work! In recovery it is said that the insanity of addiction is the addict's continuing to do the same thing while expecting a different result. The logic of cause and effect is lost on the sufferer. This is why she may be arrested repeatedly for DUI and still deny she is alcoholic. It is why he can lose multiple families and deny he is abusive. It is why she can be hospitalized several times for drug abuse and deny she is an addict.

An old joke in A.A. is that alcoholics do not have relationships, they take hostages. This is the situation for Jimmy and Doris. With Doris, the threat is inward toward herself. The chemically dependent says, directly or indirectly, "If you don't allow me to practice my disease, I'll get worse or die and it will be your fault." In the case of Jimmy, the threat is directed toward the enabler; if you do not allow me to practice my disease, I will hurt *you*. In both cases, the sufferer escapes what would be natural consequences of their behavior.

Jimmy rationalizes his violence by believing his wife does not care about him or value all he does for the family. He also believes she does not care about herself or the children—if she did, her behavior would be different. There is not a day that goes by, he thinks, in which she does not show her lack of concern for him. He becomes angry every day just anticipating uncovering evidence of this. By the time he gets home, things seem to jump out at him which prove that she does not care. He feels only physical force or physical harm can get her attention. Talking, he thinks, just elicits lies and evasions. He had a bad family as a child, where people did not care about each other, and he is *not* going to have such a family as an adult. He feels women who do not care about their husbands, children, and homes are not fit to live.

Denial of consequences provides the means of escape. The emotional bonds of marriage, the parent/child relationship, religious vows—no relationship is powerful enough to alter the course of addiction. Sue's hope that her love for Jimmy will eventually overcome his craving for violence is mistaken. Not only will his violence continue to escalate, her self-esteem will continue to dwindle, leaving her drained of love and feeling unlovable. Sue's hope that a relationship or a vow may somehow control the behavior of a chemically dependent person is an illusion, like the illusion that chains or ropes will hold the magician.

But now Sue is developing another problem. She, herself, is an adult child of chemical dependency, and unaware she has become addicted to fear. Now the thought of leaving Jimmy has become more terror-filled than the thought of staying. Sadly, Sue and the kids will stay as the violence progresses to the point where it becomes life-threatening. She will leave him then, and find someone whose disease is less dangerously progressed. As the kids grow older, they, too, become violence tolerant. If they become bored at school, they pick fights with teachers or fellow students. At home, they begin to take sides with either parent, arguing with each other over which is right, and occasionally even joining in the adult fray.

Anger addicts ultimately escape all bonds of human decency. No name is too profane to use against the other. No accusation is too outrageous to proffer. No blow is unfair to strike; everything is fair in war. Bill Wilson, the founder of Alcoholics Anonymous, was prophetic when he wrote in the book *Alcoholics Anonymous* that we who are chemically dependent cannot fight anyone or anything anymore. The powerful chemistry of resentment feeds the fires of addiction so that no addict can remain abstinent while embracing anger. And the only antidote for anger is serenity based on knowledge that a loving God will give the addict everything he needs.

In this, addicts are fortunate; despite spending a lifetime pursuing self-destruction, if they turn around to look, it is apparent that God has not abandoned them. In fact, their higher power has seen to it that even in their worst times they always, in all situations, had everything they needed. It is the addicts' experience that nothing can arrest their addiction, no human power or law, but—as the program of Alcoholics Anonymous tells us—God can and will, when sought.

CHAPTER SEVEN

Sleight-of-Hand

Sleight-of-hand is the first technique most magicians master. In this genre of tricks, the magician carefully shows you his hands—shows you there is nothing up the sleeve—and with what appear to the audience to be obvious and aboveboard moves, through sleight-of-hand produces the magical effect. In reality, while your attention was where the magician directed it, a surreptitious hand movement brought about the unexpected.

In the disease of chemical dependency, there is frequently a surreptitious motive in the most obvious and seemingly aboveboard speech and actions of the sufferer. The information she gives you may be "true," but the motive for giving it is not what it appears to be, and so, in effect, what you perceive as reality is illusion.

For instance, I knew a chemically dependent woman who told friends, employers, and physicians that her mother was dying of Alzheimer's disease, that her father was dying of lung cancer, and that she was torn between the demands of her parents, her family, and her job. This was quite true, but her motive for telling them was not what it seemed. They thought she was seeking their support in facing her difficulties. Actually, she wanted them to continue enabling her in her addiction to alcohol, tranquilizers, and sleeping pills.

Consider this situation: a client, employee, friend, or relative comes to you with numerous complaints about his spouse. She is critical, neglects the family, spends too much, is never home, is always angry, fighting with him and the kids, and her relatives are a problem. All this information may, in fact, be true, but the motive for telling it is askew, and so the sleight-of-hand is effected. You think the man wants your advice about how to handle his situation, and you may spend many hours "helping" him. (Professional counselors and clergy are particularly vulnerable to this trick!) Yet, over time you begin to notice that nothing changes for the better; rather, things continue to worsen. If you offer reasonable ideas for positive change, he comes up with reasons why they will not work or why he cannot put them in place. Eventually, *you* feel frustrated and angry. In reality the man never wanted help—never wanted things actually to get better; his motive in telling you about his marriage was to trick you into agreeing that his situation is awful and apparently hopeless. Since he chooses to maintain the destructiveness in this relationship, it is apparent that at least one drug of choice for him is adrenaline, and odds are that the spouse is also adrenaline dependent. Moreover, since addiction is a progressive disease, the intensity and frequency of the fights are likely to increase, with physical combat an eventual development. Not realizing adrenaline is an addictive chemical, you are mystified as to the man's true motivation in the situation. Sleight-of-hand is done by causing you to believe that something other than the addictive disorder is the problem.

A similar case is that of George. George's drug of choice is also adrenaline, but he creates his excitement through spending money. We mentioned George earlier. He sees need everywhere in his family and home and feels driven to satisfy it. George thinks nothing is too good for his family. There is adrenaline-producing excitement in making the purchases and also adrenaline-producing fear in knowing there isn't sufficient money to pay for them. George takes pride in never spending money on himself! At work he frequently tells coworkers about his financial problems. It is obvious from George's appearance that he in fact does spend very little on himself; consequently, coworkers believe he has serious financial problems due to the size and special needs of his family. He highlights the reality of his medical bills and the expense of college for the children. Occasionally, coworkers "lend" him money to help meet a payment or cover a check. But sometimes out in the community they notice George's wife or members of his family in cars nicer than their own and dressed better than their families and they feel uncomfortable.

Chemically dependent people use the "truth" in order to manipulate their enablers. You may run down the story and verify the facts, but the sleight-of-hand involved is related not to the facts but to the motive. The trick is to get you to support the disease process, whether it involves the use of chemicals as in the first example, or behavior as in the others. In the first case, you may be moved to encourage the poor woman with the sick parents to see her psychiatrist, who, also convinced her condition is situational, prescribes tranquilizers and sleeping pills. You may even encourage her to have a relaxing evening drink or to go out with others and "have a few drinks." Her story was designed to lead you toward making these recommendations, or at least to "understand" if she shows up a little hungover in the morning from alcohol or psychotropic drugs. Yet, if you think logically about her situation, you know that use of central nervous system depressants such as alcohol, tranquilizers, and sleeping pills actually increase depression and sleep disturbances, so such substances do not solve the problem.

In the second situation, you may encourage the sufferer to do things to gain control of his wife. If so, this is exactly what he wanted. Now he has your permission to escalate the conflict, and can tell her you told him to do so! On the other hand, when you encourage him to do something that might lead toward health, such as developing himself spiritually or examining his responsibility for his own feelings and behavior, you will quickly lose his attention. Finding his sleight-of-hand is not working, he will abandon you and search out someone more vulnerable to the trick.

George performs his sleight-of-hand by talking endlessly about his financial needs so that they seem larger than life. You do not notice they are not much different from your own. George makes life's ordinary needs seem so extraordinary that you feel compelled to assist him when he asks for a loan. If you eventually realize that George is spending inordinate amounts on unnecessary things and offer suggestions about making and keeping within a budget, you will quickly lose his "friendship," and he will move on to someone less astute. In sleight-of-hand, it is important that the audience not uncover the subterfuge. Once you have seen how the trick works, it is unlikely that you will again be drawn into supporting the surreptitious motive.

As the disease progresses, usually more than one substance/behavior of abuse is required to provide the needed neurochemical changes. Often, two or even more substances produce an effect called "synergism." In synergism, the use of more than one chemical or behavior adds up to more than the mere sum of the individual effects! There is an extra boost due to their combined use. In the first case described above, the sufferer is using alcohol, tranquilizers, and sleeping pills. In the second, the man's drug of choice is adrenaline, which he generates through fighting and extramarital relationships, both of which he justifies by his terrible marital situation. He uses some alcohol and nicotine as well. His spouse, who is also chemically dependent, uses adrenaline, sugar, fat, and complex carbohydrates. She suffers from obesity which she blames on her husband's behavior. In the third instance, George synergizes his adrenaline dependence with nicotine and caffeine.

Professional counselors such as psychiatrists, psychologists, social workers, ministers, and other therapists are extraordinarily susceptible to sleight-of-hand, spending countless hours "helping" chemically dependent people justify their disorders by believing what they present as "the problem," while missing the motive—justification for continuing the addictive behavior. Many substances and behaviors are available to alter brain chemistry. Often the less obvious remain hidden—another aspect of sleight-of-hand.

This is so in the case of bingo-loving Ethel. Unmentioned and unnoticed is the fact that each night Ethel plays bingo, she also drinks beer. Her beer consumption has risen along with her investment in bingo cards. Ethel is dependent on beer as well as bingo, but through sleight-of-hand Ethel makes everyone aware of her bingo, thus she completely hides her alcohol dependency. The flip side of this is accomplished by Jack, the alcoholic manager whose case we examined earlier. Although it causes him embarrassment, Jack highlights his drinking, which he blames on his desire to increase profits. Others see the drinking but fail to notice his addiction to adrenaline-producing stress which he exacerbates or creates for himself and others through his job. As a manager, it is easy to discover or cause stress-producing situations. His coworkers and those he supervises believe he has a drinking problem, but they primarily see him as a conscientious person who tries to perfect the product and increase their return.

As infants experiencing anger, fear, or excitement, we are introduced to adrenaline, the most likely first substance of abuse. Sugar and complex carbohydrates are typically the next mood-altering substances most of us experience, and the next substances of potential abuse. As we move into puberty, the hormones that stimulate sexual feelings are secreted and powerfully experienced. These hormones alter neurochemistry, stimulating serotonin with its resulting neurochemical cascade. Sex addiction is possibly the least identified form of chemical dependency, but it is a prevalent expression of the disease. In the case of Frank, whom we mentioned earlier, sex addiction is manifested through child molestation and incest. He also accomplishes sleight-of-hand through highlighting a problem, and by presenting himself as holy and good. Remember, Frank is the sort of man who is a leader in his church and community. He has everyone's respect. Everyone knows him as a religious person who frequently quotes scripture for others' edification. If Frank's children, or any other children whom he may encounter, tell anyone about Frank's molestation, they may not be believed and they may be punished for lying about such a respected person. Yet Frank openly claims one sin. He smokes cigarettes. He tells everyone how much he hates this weakness, and how much he wants to quit. He believes continuing to smoke represents a failure in his faith. People find this a charming flaw in such an otherwise righteous person.

So, in chemical dependency, sleight-of-hand may take the form of directing your attention to one substance or behavior of abuse, while hiding another. Many sufferers hide what they feel to be the more shameful addiction while displaying another which is more socially acceptable. A sufferer may exhibit alcoholism while hiding sexual addiction. He may talk about addiction to nicotine while hiding alcoholism. She may talk about her weight while hiding addiction to tranquilizers or anger. In the disease of chemical dependency, nothing is real, nothing is true, nothing is as it seems. The magician is always on stage, and the show is always in progress.

The magician believes herself to be just as dependent on the illusion as she is on the chemicals and behaviors. She is as driven to perform her magic as she is to practice her addiction. In her heart, she knows that without the illusion, the show will fold. In a "real" magic show, everyone understands they are being tricked, so, in effect, there is no lie, only fun. In the sleight-of-hand of chemical dependency, the illusion is intended to be perceived as reality; the lie exists even though the "truth" may be told. Illusion and reality are spiritual concepts. Illusion feeds fear; serenity is grounded in reality.

CHAPTER EIGHT

The Swords Through the Box Trick

Everyone loves the "Swords Through the Box Trick." A pretty woman gets into an empty box with just enough room for her body. The magician closes the lid. With gusto and a smile, he runs the box through, top to bottom, front to back with gleaming swords. The audience gasps! Can the girl possibly survive?

Magical addicts add a new twist to the old trick. They really run you through, then pretend they didn't. Chemically dependent magicians use swords, not of gleaming metal, but of psychological, emotional, spiritual, and sometimes physical abuse. They ignore those they are supposed to love, they lie to those whose trust they demand, they deceive those faithful to them, and they hurt those who are vulnerable. Once "run through," the sufferer, like the pretty woman in the magic show, is supposed to rise and smile, and act as if nothing happened.

Recently I was told a story involving a budding alcoholic, who was also a relationship/stress addict. He is a charming person, lovely to look at, almost perfect! He became involved with a beautiful young woman named Dana, who was in a twelve-step recovery program. He told Dana how special she was, how he had never felt this way about anyone else. But Dana heard rumors that he was still romantically involved with an old flame in another city. She asked him directly if he was still seeing this person; he adamantly denied it. Later, Dana learned that at the same time he was denying involvement with the other woman, she was, in fact, on her way to co-host an important party with him at his invitation. Even when Dana confronted him with his behavior, while admitting the woman had hosted his party, he continued to deny he had done anything wrong. His denial was so convincing that had she not been in the twelve-step program, she probably would have felt guilty for thinking he could do such a thing, and would have, along with the magical addict, pretended it never happened. Several months later, he married the other woman.

Sometimes, alcoholic magicians do not recall running us through with their swords of anger, violence, or sexually inappropriate behavior. Jack took his secretary along on one of his convention trips, telling her she worked hard and deserved to stay in a fancy hotel in a fancy city. He became intoxicated the first night and, while in a blackout, seduced her. As part of the seduction, Jack told her he had loved her for years and had a deep need for her affection. The next morning, he was mildly embarrassed to wake up in her bed. He crept out of her room and spoke to her in a polite, formal manner for the duration of the convention. Mystified and mortified, she never mentioned their night together and pretended it never happened.

Jane's children feel hurt and abandoned. Although they are in their teens and are taller than she, like baby birds larger than their parents with their mouths continually open to be fed, they still need a mother. But Jane is cross-addicted to the adrenaline her brain releases as she struggles to save her community and to Xanax. Her dependency on minor tranquilizers leaves her tired and worried about her memory. She ignores the kids unless she wants them to do something around the house or unless she needs to blame them for some behavior of her own. Actually, since chemical dependency is a progressive disease, things have been getting progressively worse; Jane began ignoring the children long ago. But she expects them to be perfectly behaved, perfectly dressed, and to have perfect grades. She tells them they are spoiled and have no right to complain; they have everything handed to them on a platter. The kids hide their abandonment and pretend everything is perfect.

Joey loves to fight with his little brother, Johnny, who is rapidly gaining a reputation as a bad boy. Actually, Joey picks on Johnny until he explodes, then loudly complains to his mom that Johnny hit him. Most recently, Joey tormented Johnny until the little one scratched his face in a fury. Then Joey gave him a powerful punch to the gut. Johnny wailed in pain, causing their mom to run to the rescue. She picked Johnny up and comforted him as he told her Joey hit him. Joey then screamed at his mom that Johnny had hurt him first, that she never cared what happened to him! He showed her the red scratches to prove it. Feeling like a terrible mother, she dropped Johnny and rushed to comfort Joey. Johnny was spanked, then made to apologize to his brother.

At night, after everyone is asleep, Frank crawls into the bed of one or the other of his children. He abuses them sexually, threatening to leave their mom if they tell. The next morning he greets the family with a cheerful smile, asking if they had a good night; everyone pretends nothing happened.

Ethel got drunk at bingo last night and insulted everyone at her table. Tonight she is back at her usual place, smiling and speaking to those she degraded the previous evening. They smile and welcome her as if nothing had happened.

Jimmy and Sue had a particularly violent night. He hit her hard enough to crack some ribs. At the emergency room, Sue tells the doctor she fell against the nightstand after tripping over a child's toy in the dark. She is sure that if she just protects Jimmy and pretends everything is fine between them one more time, he will eventually overcome his past and become a loving husband and father.

Sam's family is learning something from his ministry; they are learning that the way to get his attention is to be in crisis. The adolescent children begin acting out, becoming depressed and suicidal, abusing alcohol, and engaging in sex. His wife has also discovered interesting ways to get into trouble. They now have his undivided attention. Although they are doing life-threatening behaviors, they are all happy. In a darkly perverted way, there is nothing funnier than addiction.

Addicts protect their disease through disbelief in consequences. As we mentioned before, they never expect negative consequences. A major symptom of addiction is continuing to do the same behavior while expecting a different result. In fact, diagnosis of the disease may be made based on this symptom alone. Addicts expect the pretty young woman to step out of the box smiling and intact after they run swords through her mind, heart, and spirit. If confronted with blood, pain, and complaints, addicts are surprised and hurt, and make it appear to be the victim's fault for not doing the trick right! This craziness is real on the addict's part. A friend of mine in A.A. told me this story. He is a recovering gambler as well as a recovering alcoholic. Living in Mississippi, he disappeared from home one Friday night, not bothering to let his wife know he had decided while drunk to drive to Las Vegas. After spending several days at the gaming tables, he began the drive home without adequately supplying himself with alcohol. (Because of denial, addicts frequently minimize the amount of drug they will require, a behavior that demonstrates the reality of their denial.) Going through a dry part of Texas and detoxing, he began to feel terrible about not letting his wife know where he was. His awareness of what a miserable husband he was grew with his physical discomfort until he crossed a county line and spied a bar where he stopped. Greatly relieved after quickly downing several beers, he bought several bottles of bourbon and continued on his way. Now the drive was much more pleasant. He began to think about how much money he had won, how happy this would make his wife, and how grateful she should be to be married to such a sharp fellow.

Addicts are able to rationalize and justify *any* behavior. The neglectful mother honestly believes it is the children's job to serve her, rather than vice-versa. The incestuous father believes he is doing his children a favor by introducing them to sex in such a loving way, not leaving their sexual education to strangers. The violent man believes his wife is getting what she deserves, and therefore has no right to complain. Driven by behaviors over which they are powerless, behaviors driven by a neurochemical disorder, magical addicts go on with the show, often leaving bleeding but smiling bodies in their wake.

Extreme consequences are necessary if reality is ever to break through. The pain of consequences must outweigh the relief the addictive behavior brings. In our society, we do not handle pain well. We are taught to be sympathetic; when others hurt we hurt with them, so it is in our own interest to prevent others from hurting or to ease their pain as soon as possible if they do hurt. We are taught that pain is bad; if someone hurts we should help them get relief. While this teaching was helpful in the case of the Good Samaritan, it is not helpful in the case of addicts. In this paradox-filled disorder, preventing or lessening pain is the most dangerous, destructive thing one can do. Addicts need to be jailed when they break the law. They need to be confronted when they violate trust. They need to be left where they are when they pass out, even if it is in the car on a cold night. They need to reap any mental, psychological, biological, and spiritual consequence of their behavior short of death. Only through extremely painful or multiple painful consequences does reality crack denial, giving addicts an opportunity to see their disease and make movements toward recovery. Pain is what gives addicts and those who suffer with them a spiritual edge.

As a great saint said, if you are going to sin, sin boldly. This is because sin's consequences are painful, and great sin brings great consequences. In this universe's spiritual economy, pain is a major way God gets one's attention. And since being in relationship with God is one's greatest happiness, the chemically dependent and those who suffer with them have the opportunity to become most blessed.

CHAPTER NINE

Levitation

The stage is darkened except for a spotlight on the draped body of a voluptuous young woman lying prone on a slab in front of the magician. He stares intently at her, concentrating, focused. He runs his hands up and down over her body. Slowly, very slowly, her draped form begins to rise up off the slab. The magician has accomplished what appears to be levitation. He has defied, has negated, has reversed, has violated one of nature's basic laws, the law of gravity.

Magical addicts believe they can defy, can negate, can reverse, can violate natural law, the law of cause and effect. The fact that they absolutely do not believe, *cannot* believe in consequences, cannot be overemphasized; it is a major manifestation of the mental disorder associated with addictive disease. It is the stone foundation of denial. This disbelief in the law of cause and effect is necessary if the addict is to stay sick. So, when consequences for their behavior do occur, addicts believe they are the result of some outside, unrelated, or secondary cause; they cannot believe consequences are the direct result of addiction. When they are arrested for driving under the influence, they believe the arrest is unrighteous because the police are just on a campaign to get more money for the state or county or city by picking up people for DUI. If their spouses complain about their behavior, they believe it is because someone else has negatively influenced them, such as one of the spouse's parents or friends. If they begin suffering grave medical consequences, they deny the seriousness of the illnesses. Still bleeding from the car crash, they insist they are fine. Diagnosed with emphysema, they minimize the seriousness of the diagnosis. Having alcoholic hepatitis, they believe they can continue to drink without it turning into cirrhosis. They can become romantically involved with the spouse of a dangerous person and laugh it off when warned about possible consequences. Magical addicts believe consequences, the natural law of cause and effect, do not apply to them, and, to the amazement of those watching or involved in their performance, they seemingly defy this law night and day.

Brian is a cross-dresser. He discovered the excitement of cross-dressing several years ago. This activity led him to consciousness of, then exploration into the world of sado-masochism. For Brian, it was addiction at first experience. He fell into the masochistic side of the addiction. Brian was married. He hid his new behaviors from his spouse for a while, but she finally discovered the masochism. Brian's wife knew he was an addict—he was addicted to cocaine and was supposed to be in recovery. Brian pleaded with her to stay with him and try to understand this new behavior, saying it was really harmless and gave him the release he needed to stay sober from cocaine. His wife bought into this rationale for a while, and, in an attempt to hold her marriage together, even engaged in some punishing behavior with Brian. But in the end she was uncomfortable with the addiction and determined that Brian loved the behavior more than he loved her. When she divorced him, Brian was shocked and continued to insist, even to his lawyer, that sadomasochistic addiction was harmless. Brian told everyone, including himself, that his wife divorced him because his in-laws had unreasonably turned her against him.

Candy was surprised when she was arrested for selling methamphetamine. She believed an ex-boyfriend set her up. At her trial, she had friends and family members, even her minister, come and witness to the judge that she was really a good person. In spite of the fact that she was caught with methamphetamine-making paraphernalia in her car and had sold methamphetamine to an undercover policeman, she fully expected to get no more than probation.

Dan loves to run. He has run for years. When he goes out of town, he still runs. One of the first things he does when he goes to a new place is determine his new running route. Dan recently turned fifty years old and has had several injuries over the past few years. His doctor has told him he needs to find an exercise less stressful to his body, but he thinks his doctor is too conservative and continues to run.

In order for the disease of addiction to thrive, addicts have to convince themselves that they are so special they lie outside the normal principals of cause and effect. They *have* to believe that cigarette smoking may cause cancer in some people, but it will not cause cancer in them and that most of the talk about cigarettes causing cancer and heart attacks is just politically correct hype anyway. After all, they know people who are ninety years old and still smoking cigarettes. And who wants to live to be ninety anyway? And everyone has to die of something; life is something no one survives.

Even though they may *say* everyone has to die of something, addicts never, ever expect consequences, certainly not *real* consequences that have life altering effects. Addicts expect some fairly minor problems as a result of their behavior, some disgruntlement from others with which they have to contend, complaints that are fairly easily deflected. They expect minor illnesses, minor accidents, and manageable legal problems. But they never, ever expect divorce or serious illness or death or imprisonment.

After his divorce, Brian pursued his addictive behaviors and pretty soon relapsed into cocaine use once more. His parents put him into treatment repeatedly, but while he was willing to admit the cocaine was a problem, he was never able to admit the sadomasochistic behavior was a problem. He insisted this behavior harmed no one and held that any sexual behavior entered into by mutually consenting adults could not be faulted. This behavior of his was not a manifestation of addictive disease, he contended, because it was harmless. Brian would become abstinent from cocaine, continue the sexual behavior, relapse on cocaine, and re-enter treatment at the insistence of his parents. He repeated this behavior over and over and over, because no one could convince him the sexual piece was either addictive or harmful. Soon after leaving his last treatment, Brian was accidentally killed in one of his masochistic pursuits. His parents were glad he was "in recovery" and cocaine-free.

In spite of what they say, those who engage in sex addiction as a manifestation of their disease *always* believe what they do is wrong or harmful. If they did not believe this, they would not find the behavior interesting. No one can become addicted to "normal" sex with a spouse. In order for sexual behavior to be addictive, it must have an element of risk, it must in some way be "bad." The sex addict is not addicted to the biochemistry that normal sexual activity produces. Sex addicts become addicted to fight/flight biochemistry, the biochemistry of stress. They use aberrant sexual behavior to activate stress chemistry. And since sex addiction, like all other expressions of addictive behavior, is progressive, the behavior must over time become more and more risky, more and more dangerous, for the addict to get the fix he needs.

Candy received a three-year prison sentence. She, her family, even her minister were shocked. She, along with her family, friends, and minister, thought the judge had perpetrated a terrible injustice! They have called the ex-boyfriend's family to tell them how awful it is that the ex-boyfriend set Candy up like this.

Dan's knee went out. He had to have surgery. Before he fully recovered, he was running again. He had to have more surgery. Now he has a disabled sticker on his license plate and may never fully recover. Dan believes his doctor botched the job on the surgeries. He looks forward to going back to running soon.

When serious consequences occur, they may so surprise and disorient the addict that the illusion of immunity from the natural law of cause and effect is broken and the addict momentarily enters the real world. When this happens, there is a small window of opportunity to intervene to get them into treatment, into recovery. However, the window is small, and the opportunity is short-lived, because the addict will almost immediately discover how to misinterpret the consequence, making it seem less serious than it is and making it someone else's fault.

God puts consequences in place to get our attention, to show us we are headed in the wrong direction. For the addict, consequences are the only things that can bring about conversion, deliver us into a new life, bring about our re-birth, save us from the further progression of the disease. When well-meaning people deflect or absorb these consequences, they only succeed in making future consequences more painful, more dangerous, more serious. Consequences are God's gift to the addict.

CHAPTER TEN

Strange Sustenance

One of the most subtle and seldom recognized forms of addiction is addiction to anger. Bill Wilson and Dr. William D. Silkworth developed the first enlightened addiction theory over fifty years ago. They understood addiction to be a disease of the body, mind, and spirit. Knowing nothing of neurochemistry at the time, Dr. Silkworth described the alcoholic's unique response to alcohol as an allergy. He recognized even then that alcoholics react to alcohol differently than do nonalcoholics. Bill Wilson did not understand the chemistry of anger, but he saw clearly that anger and resentment represent the greatest danger to the recovery of alcoholics, and that alcoholics cling to anger and resentment longer than those who do not suffer from the disease. This was a remarkable insight for the time, and now, fifty years later, we are just beginning to understand adrenaline as a body-produced drug of abuse for those who suffer from chemical dependency. Adrenaline alters neurochemistry both through elevating blood sugar and insulin and through direct action at the site of receptor neurons, creating a synergistic effect. When the neurotransmitter serotonin and adrenaline co-occur at the receptor, the signal is much stronger. It is like turning up the volume on your telephone receiver. And adrenaline in combination with other neurotransmitters triggered by anger and resentment is highly addictive.

Anger is *always* a symptom of fear, fear that we will not get what we need or want, or fear that we will lose something we have. The feeling we perceive as anger is the result of surging adrenaline and other body-produced chemicals that prepare us for either fight or flight whenever we are afraid. Fear is frequently perceived as anger; we find anger a more acceptable emotion. It is far more acceptable to the ego to say "he made me mad" instead of "he frightened me." But nevertheless, however righteous or justified, anger is always fear.

In our society, a primary fear concerns loss of face or self-esteem. We are afraid to confront others, afraid of being confronted, afraid we do not measure up, afraid to speak in public, afraid we will not fit in, afraid we are not smart enough, thin enough, strong enough, handsome/pretty enough, rich enough, educated enough, or well-connected enough. We are afraid others will not like us, love us, respect us, fear us. Our other primary fear is that of loss of control. Our inability to control people, places, and things to meet needs or guarantee safety produces fear in all but the most deeply spiritual. Since many areas of life are beyond our control, those prone to addictive disease are at risk of becoming dependent on stress's biochemistry. Once dependent, not only do we respond to stressful events that come our way naturally, we learn to precipitate stress. And since addiction is a progressive disorder, over time we find we must increase our stress to meet our body's increasing tolerance.

Many children of chemically dependent parents are thrill-seekers and risk-takers, meaning they seek out and create adrenaline-producing activities. They play hard and are often injured. They run into the street without looking, climb too high in trees and go out on limbs, skate recklessly, and ride their bikes dangerously. They enjoy taking risks, both physical and psychological, and may provoke fistfights and arguments. They challenge authority provocatively and brag about being in trouble. They often lie, even when telling the truth would be easier; lies always produce a little adrenaline release. If brought to a mental health professional, they are often diagnosed with oppositional defiant disorder, but if someone took the trouble to look underneath the behavior, they would find profound sadness and depression.

As these children mature, they frequently combine substances with thrill-seeking, risk-taking behavior, often beginning with nicotine, alcohol, and automobiles. They drink and drive, speed, or otherwise threaten the lives of themselves and others in vehicles. Frequently they are absent from school and often in verbal altercations with authority figures. At home, they rage over inconsequential matters and resist parental controls. They are verbally abusive to the family and may become physically so. In more extreme cases, and with increased substance abuse, parents and siblings may be physically at risk. And they are just as powerless over this behavior as any adult addict is over the use of chemicals. Attempts to appease or please these sufferers are futile, since their need is not to be at peace, but at war. When fighting, they secrete sufficient adrenaline to sustain comfortable neurochemistry. The unrecovering chemically dependent adult or child is often faced with only two feeling choices: anger or depression. Of these, anger is the better feeling and will usually prevail.

As young children, those who are predisposed to the neurochemistry of chemical dependency frequently discover three substances that change their feelings in the direction of comfort. One is adrenaline. The others are sugar and caffeine. Caffeine is usually discovered in childhood in the wonderful combination of fat and sugar called chocolate, or combined with sugar in soft drinks. Many children of chemically dependent parents prefer sugar and complex carbohydrates over adrenaline. These young people may avoid risk-taking activities. In fact, they may avoid most activities. They spend their time snacking, and snacks are their constant companions. But as the disease progresses, most sufferers learn they must combine several mechanisms to alter brain chemistry. As they grow into adulthood and require more neuronal stimulation, they, too, often turn to adrenaline. The "jolly fat man" is frequently a very fearful person. Sufferers whose drug of choice is carbohydrates may continue in their passive role, but obtain adrenaline stimulation vicariously through the exciting activities of those around them. They may become soap opera addicts, pursuing the lives of others either through involvement with family, friends, coworkers, or characters on the TV screen. Some of them become psychotherapists.

As a drug of choice, fear is cheap and easy to come by. People can fear almost anything, since they may either fear they will not get what they need or want, or fear they may lose what they have. Not only are we fearful during waking hours, while sleeping we experience fearful dreams which alter our brain chemistry. Adrenaline is a drug always available in an almost inexhaustible supply. And adrenaline addiction is also an easy addiction to hide; others seldom expect someone to want to be angry or fearful. Anger simultaneously provides the addict with a "free" drug of choice, an excuse to use other chemicals, and a smoke screen in which to disappear after firing a barrage of blame at others for the anger. It is truly a magic potion. But like all magic potions, it backfires.

The excitement produced by a delightful challenge or opportunity is healthy. Such excitement causes a neurochemistry that is quite different from that of fear. The neurochemistry produced by fear fires wars at home and abroad, between nation and nation, husband and wife, child and parent, brother and sister, friend and friend. It stifles love and sours relationships. It destroys households and empires. It devours dreams and creativity. It kills both the body and the soul.

Fear is at the center; it is the very core of all spiritual sickness—fear that I will not get what I need or want, or that I will lose what I have. There are several emotional states which are wholly incompatible; fear cannot abide with love—"love casts it out!" (1 John 4:18). So the spiritual must be at the core of any recovery process involving chemical dependency. One may be "dry" or "clean" without the spiritual, but one cannot be at peace without the spiritual. Serenity is not a negative state; it's a state of freedom from the bondage of fear, a condition in which one can become fully one's self. Because of the addict's disordered neurochemistry, peace is essential to worthwhile and lasting recovery.

Addiction extorts a terrible cost, the loss of both peace and the genuine ability to love. This same price is demanded of those in close relationship with the addict as well. In the following chapter, we will examine just how high this price may be.

CHAPTER ELEVEN

Admission

There is an admission charge for every magic show; the better the show, the more you must pay the magician. Relationships with the chemically dependent are costly, too. The further the disease progresses, the higher the price.

One cost of living with illusion is loss of sleep. An inability to go to bed and go to sleep is a chronic problem in chemically dependent families. Control is a central issue in these families, and going to sleep feels like capitulation. Not only do the parents stay up all hours, vaguely fearing that they will miss something or something may happen, but the children often stay up as well. Loss of sleep causes mental confusion and depression and also weakens the immune system. Chronic illnesses plague chemically dependent families, in part directly due to loss of sleep. Impaired sleep also leads to serious accidents.

Another loss which may always be expected in chemically dependent relationships is that of income. You will either/or: pay for the chemicals/behaviors of abuse, take up the monetary slack caused by the sufferer's use of the chemicals/behaviors, pay to get him out of trouble caused by the use, pay for things she lost or destroyed as a result of the abuse, pay to get him in/

out of hospitals and jails, and pay for your own resulting illness and medical treatment. You may lose income because of days lost from work in order to "help" her. You may lose jobs because you are so consumed with concern about him that you are unable to concentrate, just marking time at work until you can get free to control the addict's behavior. But while important, loss of sleep and money are minor concerns compared to other costs associated with chemically dependent relationships. They include peace of mind, time, self-esteem, and the ability to love.

It is hard to set a price on peace of mind; without deep, spiritual grounding, peace of mind is always lost in a relationship with one who suffers from addiction. In a magic show, you pay to be surprised and fooled. In a ninety-minute performance, this is fun, but never knowing what to expect next from the chemically dependent, attempting to anticipate and control the unpredictable, uncontrollable behavior of the addict, invites emotional exhaustion. Planning the outcome in a complex system such as human behavior is impossible, yet codependents engage in a chase-your-tail/merry-go-round of obsession—thinking "if he does this, I'll do that" and "I'll do this before she does that." Fear and worry are constant companions of all the family members—fear that they will not get what they need or will lose what they have as well as fear of and for the addict. Loss of peace of mind has its own set of consequences, including stress-related illnesses such as cardiovascular disease and damage to the immune system. The ramifications of loss of peace of mind are far-reaching for each family member; besides ill health and increased accidents, each member suffers loss of emotional energy for other relationships.

The first relationships to go are friendships. Then, more emotional energy is spent trying to control the addict so that there is none left for the extended family. As fear becomes more pervasive, no emotional energy is available for the immediate family. At this point, a bizarre reversal occurs; young children, seeing their parents' emotional needs, try to take on the parental role. For a time, the children attempt to become emotional stabilizers for the parents. But their efforts are doomed, and gradually each individual closes up in a cocoon of fear, isolating themselves from each other and finally even from themselves. The idea of being isolated from oneself seems strange to the uninitiated, but it is a condition familiar to chemically dependent families. Self-isolation involves not knowing what you, yourself, are feeling; not really knowing what you, yourself, are thinking; not being able to communicate with yourself; not being able to make sense in your own mind.

Chronic fear leads to loss of time, and time does not come cheap. Even though you may have some emotional energy left, if you spend all your time worrying/wondering about the chemically dependent, you lose all your other relationships simply because you do not have time for them. If every minute is spent trying to control or planning to control the sufferer and her environment, you have no time for children, family, friends, or yourself. You become so consumed with the sufferer you have no time to dress carefully, buy clothes and toiletries, exercise, eat properly, or recreate. You believe someday your efforts will be rewarded, someday you will figure out the tricks and prevail over the magician; then you will have time for the children, the rest of the family, your friends, and yourself. Of course, without a powerful intervention, this does not happen, and time contraction becomes an all-consuming downward spiral. The more time you invest in controlling the addict the more you lose; the more you lose, the more you invest. Of course, you will have no primary relationship with the chemically dependent, because all their relationships are secondary. In the meantime, life rushes by. Children grow up. Parents die. Friends change their interests. A joke in codependency circles is that when a codependent dies, someone else's life flashes before his eyes. Living someone else's life robs you of the time to relate personally and lovingly to others and yourself.

Another cost is self-esteem. Maintaining self-esteem while in relationship with one who is chemically dependent is next to impossible. Only a person with a highly developed spirituality can maintain such a relationship and hold on to their sense of self-worth. The chemically dependent tells you your self-worth is directly related to your ability to make him happy, so you begin to value yourself based on how successful you are at this. But for the chemically dependent, unhappiness is the result of disordered brain chemistry. Because of the disease, only a change in neurochemistry brings addicts the relief they require, and prior to recovery this change only comes through the use of substances and behaviors of abuse. In the long run, all efforts to please those who are chemically dependent meet with failure. So if you place your self-worth on your ability to make a sufferer happy, your self-esteem will continually shrink; ultimately this becomes a self-propagating descent into despair.

The more you try to please a sufferer—to help him—the more of your own esteem you invest in being successful. The more you try to please, the more obvious it becomes that you are failing. The chemically dependent tells you to try harder, that you are failing because you do not care about him. So you try harder. Your self-worth plunges into the abyss.

The loss of self-worth is always accompanied by the most awful cost of relationship with the chemically dependent, the loss of the ability to love. Love given only with the expectation of a return is not love at all—it is self-interest. In relationship with a sufferer, you are continually told that love is conditional; she will love you when you make her happy. In other words, she will love you as long as you help her pursue the chemicals/behaviors of abuse. You are told that to show love, you must allow and support the sufferer's self-destruction. Living in this mad wonderland where bad is good and right is wrong, your own idea of love becomes distorted. You begin to believe you are incapable of love since you can never seem to satisfy the addict's demands. In your confusion, you, too, begin to believe that if someone doesn't make you happy he does not love you. Since no one *does* make you happy, and because your self-worth is so compromised, you become sure no one loves you. Because you accept the addict's convincing illusion that love means making another person happy (giving her what she wants) you, too, lose your ability to love and be loved.

The situation would indeed be hopeless if it were not for the spiritual. Like a movie about an evil magician, if the heroine cries out for help, the spiritual is quick to save. And when the mirrors crack and the smoke clears, everything that was lost is returned, with interest.

CHAPTER TWELVE

The Smoke Clears

Caught up in illusion, the chemically dependent and those who suffer with them continue on their course of destruction. Illusion is so pervasive in the lives of sufferers, the magical addicts themselves become fooled. Like people lost in a glass house at a fair, they are trapped again and again by what appears to be the way out. This glass house was designed by an evil magician; there is no exit. Sufferers work themselves deeper and deeper into the illusion. Their only escape is into reality.

In an old *Star Trek* episode, the crew suddenly found themselves in Tombstone, Arizona, at the time of the gunfight at the OK Corral. Dressed in western attire with six-shooters strapped to their legs, they were drawn into the tensions and, ultimately, the fight. One of them was killed. Mr. Spock, through his lack of human emotion, discovered this was all an illusion, a show set up by some alien beings; if they did not believe in what appeared to be happening, nothing could harm them. The rest of the crew was sure that they must fight to stay alive. Spock had to convince them the bullets they saw flying through the air and seeming to kill their friends were not real. There was danger only if they believed the illusion. To escape into reality the others had to trust Spock, although their eyes and minds told them he was the deluded one!

Sufferers from chemical and codependency need a "higher power" such as Spock provided in the *Star Trek* episode to escape from their illusion. Blinded by the human emotions of fear and hopelessness, they are unable to see the route readily open to them. Bill Wilson, in the book *Alcoholics Anonymous,* puts it this way: "Our description of the alcoholic, the chapter to the agnostic, and our personal adventures before and after (recovery) make clear three pertinent ideas:

(a) That we were alcoholic and could not manage our own lives.

(b) That probably no human power could have relieved our alcoholism.

(c) That God could and would if He were sought."*

Spirituality is not an arbitrary component of recovery, so that we can take it or leave it. Spirituality is the *core* of recovery. Only through belief in a higher power can we turn our wills and lives over to this power, escaping from fear, anger, and resentment. As long as we are fearful, angry, and resentful we cannot become abstinent from adrenaline, which when combined with other biochemicals associated with anger is one of the most powerful addictive chemicals, and recovery will continue to elude us! Recovery is not a negative condition in which we abstain from alcohol and drugs, although abstinence is a necessary component

---

* From *Alcoholics Anonymous The Big Book,* p. 60. ©1939, 1955, 1976, 2001 by Alcoholics Anonymous World Services, Inc., New York. Used with permission.

of recovery. Recovery is a progression toward peace, freedom, and happiness.

Just as those of us who are chemically dependent react differently to alcohol, sugar, complex carbohydrates, and other drugs, we also react differently to adrenaline. For us, indulging in fear and anger is the same as taking a drink or snorting cocaine. Adrenaline triggers the addictive process, which includes craving for our other drugs of choice. The angry abstinent alcoholic will not be abstinent for long. The resentful cocaine addict will not stay drug-free. The self-pitying carbohydrate craver will not be able to maintain abstinence. The fearful sex addict will act out. Human beings are limited, finite creatures endowed with the ability to foresee the possibility of loss of any of the people, places, and things they believe they need to be happy. They foresee disease and the inevitability of death. Anxiety and fear are unavoidable without belief and trust in a loving, omnipotent, and omniscient higher power. Only the spiritual can bring the peace, freedom, and happiness necessary for long-term recovery. The spiritual leads us away from deception and toward truth.

Seen through the eyes of eternity, loss, disease, and death are not the ultimate reality; they have no more power to wound permanently than the bullets in the old *Star Trek* episode.

The evil magician tells us everything is serious and dangerous. We are led to believe we are alone in an unfriendly world where we must struggle and fight to stay alive, just like the crew in *Star Trek*. For this reason, everything seems personal; every sentence has an "I" in it. (A little known but much hated and tiresome experience of the chemically dependent and those who suffer with them is the constant mental use of the pronoun "I"; I need, I think, I know, I want, I should, I have got to, I feel, I hurt, I am angry, I am scared, I am lonely, I am miserable, and on and on in an endless procession of I's. The mental use of "I" is so pervasive that a major way to tell if recovery is working is to check out whether the proliferation of mental I's has diminished.)

How can we come to believe that loss, disease, suffering, and death are not serious and that we do not need to fear them when the Evil Magician assures us they are real? The world taught us to take things seriously. As children, we were chided for not taking things seriously enough. Now we hear about a spirituality that tells us what we considered real is really illusion and not to be taken seriously; we are invited to believe we are protected and loved by an omniscient, loving power greater than ourselves. This wonderful spirituality assures us we will get *everything* we need by trusting in this higher power. How can we believe this? But if we do not, how can we be relieved of our fear? And, if we are not relieved from fear, we will continue on our path to destruction. What a dilemma!

The paradox of recovery is that we win by surrendering. I have been a chemical dependency counselor for many years. I have never seen anyone overcome chemical or codependency who did not first give up. Only complete defeat can interrupt the struggle for control. In defeat, we surrender. When we surrender, fear subsides. Have you ever seen one animal being killed by another? First, there is a valiant struggle while the animal's body pumps adrenaline, empowering it to fight or flee. However, once the victim realizes the attacking animal has overcome it, it seems to relax and gives up the struggle.

This must happen to us in order to escape from illusion. We have to admit powerlessness over all our dependencies and our fears, and admit that our lives are unmanageable, uncontrollable. Once we give up trying to control ourselves and others, trying to meet our needs and protect ourselves, then we may open our minds to the possibility of help from a power greater than ourselves. As long as we struggle, trusting in our own power or that of other human beings, the fear that we are in danger rightly continues. Once we admit we are powerless over people, places, and things—loss, illness, life, and death—our minds tend to open to the possibility of the spiritual. Interestingly, this is all the higher power needs to deliver us from illusion. It happens automatically. All we need to experience our higher power is an open mind!

All my life as a Christian I had been taught I had to have faith. I pursued faith as though it were a commodity, like pork bellies or gold, thinking if somehow I got enough of it I would get anything I wanted. In Alcoholics Anonymous I learned the reverse was true. Faith was a gift I received when I stopped pursuing it and opened my mind. And faith meant a conscious, direct relationship with my higher power. I could know and do God's will for me; the greatest freedom lay in doing what I should do because I wanted to do it.

Like Job, in order to know God rather than knowing about God, all we have to do is reject everything we thought we knew and open our minds. Once delusion is shattered, the walls of the glass house disappear. We discover we have been sustained all the time, even while we did our best to destroy our health, emotions, and spirits. We realize we have been protected and loved all along by a power greater than ourselves; that all along we have always had exactly what we needed.

In this disease, we at first think the chemically dependent is the evil and powerful magician. My first husband was chemically dependent, and I believed he was the problem. As time passed, it became apparent that I, too, suffered from the disease and acted like an evil magician. In recovery, I realized that both my husband and I had been deluded by the real evil magician—the disease itself! In recovery from this disease, the distinction between the chemically dependent and the codependent fades like the magician's smoke. We all discover that our common primary difficulty is fear; fear that we will not get what we think we need or will lose what we have. Our disordered brain chemistry tells us we will die if we do not use chemicals or behaviors to alter it and we are afraid we will not be able to get and use them. Codependency tells us we must control the uncontrollable to survive. Chemically dependent people are always codependent, and codependent people are usually chemically dependent, with at least one of the chemicals of choice being fear-produced adrenaline! Seldom have I seen a codependent person who was not genetically predisposed to chemical dependency through family history.

Recovery says this fear is a delusion. We will not die without chemicals; rather it is the chemicals and behaviors that will kill us. Recovery tells us that since we have a chronic, metabolic disease, we will at times feel depressed, irritable, or anxious, but these feelings will pass and are not life-threatening. Recovery tells the codependent that God loves the chemically dependent much more than the codependent does, and is far better equipped to take care of them. Like the *Star Trek* episode at the OK Corral, chemical dependency is powerless to harm us once stripped of the terrifying illusion it creates. With our lives in the hands of our higher power there is *really* nothing to fear. *Nothing can separate us from this love.*

Epilogue

The following is a summary of the Twelve Steps of Alcoholics Anonymous. The steps themselves came from A.A.* The summaries were adapted by the author from her book *12 Steps to Loving Yourself,* published by Forward Movement, and are printed with permission.

From the beginning, A.A.'s founder Bill Wilson hoped others outside A.A. would find these steps helpful. Indeed, due to the success people experience using these steps, many other groups have appropriated them. They outline a "simple" program with profound results. The program promises serenity, freedom from fear of people and economic insecurity, and a new happiness. Anyone who embarks on this spiritual journey while maintaining rigorous honesty will be amazingly blessed. Following the steps, you find you get everything you need, and that what you get is what you wanted all the time.

Step One—We admitted we were powerless over [*fill in blank*], that our lives had become unmanageable.

Because of pride, we go on, sometimes endlessly, trying to control the things that are troubling in our lives. Usually we blame people, places, and things for our problems, exerting ourselves mightily to change things to meet our needs. These days there is much talk of "empowerment," but the reality is

---

* From *Alcoholics Anonymous The Big Book,* p. 59-60. ©1939, 1955, 1976, 2001 by Alcoholics Anonymous World Services, Inc., New York. Used with permission.

that other people, places, and things are, for the most part, independent of our control. No matter how assertive or even aggressive we become, they continue, like tides and planets, on their own course. Unhappily, no matter how much willpower we throw at these things, they don't conform to our desires. As a last resort, we try changing these people, places, and things altogether through geographic cures, divorces, and job moves, yet our distress follows us. Working Step One, we halt this endless process by acknowledging our powerlessness.

Although one is an extension of the other, this step has two distinct parts: we admit both powerlessness and unmanageability. Sometimes we admit powerlessness, but deny that we are affected by it. For instance, I may acknowledge powerlessness over anger, depression, anxiety, my child, food, my boss, my spouse, or my finances, but I will not admit this bothers me; I pretend to go on with my life as though nothing were wrong. Yet to get well, I must admit the pain in my situation cripples me, and that powerlessness is, by definition, unmanageability. Coming into agreement with reality, I can prepare to let go of my attempts to control the uncontrollable. Pride is unwilling to admit complete defeat, but humility is the key that opens me up to experience the power of God's love.

Step Two—Came to believe that a Power greater than ourselves could restore us to sanity.

A mind that is not open to belief in a higher power will lead to despair. Looking honestly at the unmanageability of my life, with my illusion of control shattered, I appear to be undefended in a hopeless situation. At this point, I may not believe in God, or I may not trust the God I was taught to believe in. Perhaps I feel unworthy of God's help. But I see the Twelve Step program bringing results, seemingly miraculous results, to others. The program tells me all I need is an open mind to experience God. All I need to do is exchange doubt and disbelief for openness. I am told that pride of intellect, pride of self-sufficiency, pride of unworthiness (telling God whom to love), and pride of defiance can all be overcome through the simple process of opening the mind. I discover that either in or out of prayer I have always sought my own will; I have never unconditionally said, "Thy will be done." Emptying my mind of all demands and preconceptions, I meet God.

Step Three—Made a decision to turn our will and our lives over to the care of God *as we understood God.*

"Nothing has changed, but everything is different." This is an expression that describes the experience of making the decision described in Step Three. The decision is a spiritual action wherein having come to believe in a living, loving God with whom we can be in relationship and whose power is greater than ours, we give up our own unhappy and unsuccessful struggle to run the show for ourselves and others. We turn over our whole selves—physical, intellectual, emotional, and spiritual—to the God of our understanding. We can only turn in this way to the God we understand; God as revealed to us in Step Two. It is only the God we understand that we can trust with every facet of our lives and the lives of those we love.

Step Four—Made a searching and fearless moral inventory of ourselves.

Step Four can be successfully attempted only after taking Steps Two and Three. Only after turning our lives over to a loving God and living to tell about it can we take a "searching and fearless moral inventory of ourselves." Until now, we made searching moral inventories of others. If the searchlight turned on ourselves, we rationalized, minimized, and blamed people, places, and things for our shortcomings. Working Step Four, for the first time we eliminate blame from our spiritual vocabulary and accept responsibility for our character defects. Taking this step represents another giant step into reality and humility. Unless we recognize our character defects and take responsibility for them, we can make no further spiritual progress.

We are surprised to discover that the sources of our emotional insecurities—worry, anger, self-pity, and depression—are our own character defects rather than the fault of people, places, and things. We find that our own defenses have ambushed us spiritually and emotionally. The rewards for a thorough Step Four are self-acceptance, confidence, and rightened relationships. When we stop blaming others and take responsibility for our own defensiveness, our relationships improve.

Step Five—Admitted to God, to ourselves, and to another human being the exact nature of our wrongs.

Step Five is one of the three most difficult steps and therefore is one of the most freeing. The sports adage of "no pain, no gain" works in the realm of the spirit, as well. This twelve-step path leads progressively toward greater humility, which opens us increasingly to God's grace. Both the church and secular society understand the need for and benefits of confession, whether through priest, psychiatrist, friend, or counselor. An old counseling adage is that we are only as sick as our secrets. Without admitting the details of our worst character defects to another person, we never receive the peace of mind the steps promise. Careful choice of the person in whom to confide is important. A counselor or minister may be best, someone professionally committed to confidentiality.

The benefits of the step are as wonderful as taking the step is terror-filled.

They include the ability to accept and give forgiveness, a feeling of kinship with the rest of the world, increased honesty and, thus, tranquility, a new ability to love ourselves, and oneness with God.

Step Six—Were entirely ready to have God remove all these defects of character.

In Step Six we grow in our awareness that our character defects, our defenses, are the source of our difficulties. We more profoundly understand that it is not what others do that disturbs us; it is our own fear that our needs will not be met that causes our emotional distress. We are angry, worried, and depressed because we fear we will not get what we need physically and emotionally, and our egos will not be validated, satisfying our need for self-esteem. This is why we violate our values through dishonest people-pleasing. Now we have turned our lives—physical, emotional, and spiritual—over to a loving God, from whom we get our validation. Since our defenses have become superfluous, we are entirely ready to have God remove them. Steps Two onward represent the beginning of a lifelong process that is never completed, but we can continue to make spiritual progress. The more we root out our defeating defenses and trust God, the freer we become and the more peace and joy we experience.

Step Seven—Humbly asked Him to remove our short-comings.

As we make spiritual progress by trusting God and taking responsibility for our fears, we discover we are powerless over our character defects and need God's help to remove them. We begin to understand on a more profound level that it is in God we "live, and move, and have our being" (Acts 17:28), and without God we can do nothing. It is from God that we get our physical strength, our capacity to feel, think, work, and play. We begin to recognize that we did not write, produce, or direct life's play—we did not even buy a ticket to the show! We humbly ask God to remove our defects and defenses. As Alcoholics Anonymous says, in Step Seven we move even more "out of ourselves and toward God."

Step Eight—Made a list of all persons we had harmed, and became willing to make amends to them all.

The goal of the following two steps is, based on our new understanding of ourselves, to develop the best possible relationship with every human being we know.

This is another step that we never complete, but it is vitally important for our spiritual growth and peace of mind that we begin. In this step we only make our list and become willing. We are not yet ready to make amends.

Step Eight is a three-part step, and the second part cannot be well begun until the first part is underway. We may become embarrassed if we attempt to make amends before we are spiritually mature enough to do so. Yet one of A.A.'s sayings about this step as well as all the others is "easy does it, but darn it, do it!"

The first part of Step Eight has to do with forgiveness. Often the people we have harmed are those we believe harmed us; we cannot ask for forgiveness from them until we forgive them. We realize we have been dealing with fellow sufferers who acted out of fear and emotional instability, and we see that our mutual defenses have fed each others' distress. Having done a thorough Step Four, we are no longer self-righteous and understand that compared to our loving higher power, no one is righteous.

The second part includes defining "harm." Harm done to others includes physical, mental, emotional, and/or spiritual damage, and involves "sins" of omission as well as commission. A rule of thumb is that anyone with whom we were angry we probably harmed; anyone whom we do not want to see or talk to we have probably harmed. In the story of the prodigal son, the father sees his erring son coming toward home but still far away, and joyfully runs to meet him (before he apologizes). This showed not only his forgiveness of the son but also demonstrated the father's innocence toward the son. Anyone we would prefer to avoid we have probably harmed.

The third part of the step is willingness. We must become willing to make amends to them all.

The benefits include greater peace, partnership, and fellowship with men and women and with God.

Step Nine—Made direct amends to such people wherever possible, except when to do so would injure them or others.

This is the second of the three hardest steps. Most other steps are done inwardly, so we can sometimes fool ourselves that we have done them. This is an action step which involves others as witnesses to the reality of our humility.

Many have become confused about the words "except when to do so would injure them or others." Often in meetings I have heard it said that "I am one of the others not to be hurt in taking the ninth step." Sometimes this represents fear and/or unwillingness to make the amends. It must be only out of love that we make the decision not to make amends, not for selfish reasons. We make the amends, not the offended person; while it is fortunate if the offended accepts our amends, that is not necessary for the program to work and for us to reap its benefits. What is important is that we open ourselves, not that the gesture is returned.

If amends are not made in a timely fashion, we make no further spiritual progress. This step demonstrates our willingness to take responsibility for our actions, to trust God to provide the spiritual and physical resources to make the amends, and represents a great spiritual leap—the willingness to take responsibility for the well-being of others. Here we feel fear slip away, as predicted in the promises, and experience true peace of mind.

Step Ten—Continued to take personal inventory and when we were wrong promptly admitted it.

The goal of all these steps is increased humility, making more room for God's grace, increasing God's peace and power in our lives. Humility is not degrading; it is an honest, realistic view of ourselves in relation to God and our fellows. In our old, defensive mode, we strove for perfection, expecting it in ourselves and others. We admitted only the faults or errors we did not care too much about, so we would not appear arrogant. We burned with shame if we were caught in a mistake, and denied, blamed, and rationalized it in an attempt to defend ourselves, making Step Ten the last of the three most difficult steps. Now that we know we have God's approval, that God counts us righteous through God's own will and action rather than because of our efforts, we can acknowledge our mistakes right away and make amends where called for. This is another important step into reality.

Taking our daily inventory, there will also be things we have done well. We begin to see God's grace in our lives. Maybe we held our tongue when we wanted to gossip. We may have had the grace to give someone a real compliment. Perhaps we enjoyed playing with our children or listening to our spouse's conversation. We move beyond tolerance toward true love for our neighbor (whoever is nearby).

Step Eleven—Sought through prayer and meditation to improve our conscious contact with God as *we understood God*, praying only for knowledge of God's will for us and the power to carry that out.

The implication of Step Eleven: God is alive and we can have a personal relationship with God. We began and broadened this relationship throughout the steps. As our awareness of God's grace grows, our desire for a closer relationship increases. We find that prayer and meditation quiet the noise in our minds and souls, making a more direct relationship possible.

Through our pursuit of the steps, we found God knows all about us, but we knew little about God. We were told things by our parents, or perhaps our church; maybe we read some things. But in the past, like Job, we had only heard; now we know. Now we have a direct relationship with God as a result of humbling ourselves to accept God's will for us. We do not get into theological arguments with anyone.

Yet, since we are still fallible and willful people (we claim progress, not perfection), we need anchors to keep us from floating adrift and following other voices. Self-will often dresses up as God's "still, small voice." Sources of meditation many of us in recovery find to be helpful include the prayer attributed to Saint Francis, the Sermon on the Mount, the Summary of the Law (Love God with all your heart and your neighbor as yourself), and the biblical Letter of James. There are forms of meditation that are less than helpful; we need to be sure whose spirit we are invoking!

We pray only for knowledge of God's will and the power to carry it out. In the past we scarcely knew what was good for us, so we find it presumptuous to ask for specifics for ourselves or others. As we experience God's increasing love in our lives, we learn to trust that all things work together for good for those who love God; we find he is the best judge of what is good for us.

Step Twelve—Having had a spiritual awakening as the result of these steps, we tried to carry this message to alcoholics, and to practice these principles in all our affairs.

Here are some of Bill W.'s words about the Twelfth Step: "When a man or a woman has a spiritual awakening, the most important meaning of it is that he has now become able to do, feel, and believe that which he could not do before on his unaided strength and resources alone....He has been set on a path which tells him he is really going somewhere, that life is not a dead end, not something to be endured or mastered. In a very real sense he has been transformed because he has laid hold of a source of strength which, in one way or another, he had hitherto denied himself. He finds himself in possession of a degree of honesty, tolerance, unselfishness, peace of mind, and love of which he had thought himself quite incapable."*

These are qualities that cannot be hidden. And they are very attractive! People will want what you have! You will carry the message in your living as well as in your conversation, as you "practice these principles." But there will also be many who believe your message is foolishness, that you just do not understand the real world. How deluded they are, just as you were! These steps are not for everyone who needs them, but for anyone who wants them. There will be those who want them.

As we practice these principles, we continually come back to the first step and repeat the cycle with more profound understanding, greater freedom, and increasing happiness.

To Work—Find partners to work the steps.

Working the steps alone is only slightly better than not working them at all. One of the first, sure signs of humility, the quality we are pursuing, is to recognize we need help in developing the honesty required to work the steps. Working them with others, or at least another, is far preferable to attempting to

---

work them alone. These steps should not be worked with family members or people with whom we have an interdependent relationship. Partners in working the steps need a degree of objectivity and independence if they are to be truly helpful to each other.

Find a partner who wants to work the steps, but who does not share your character defects. Find someone who will help you see through your delusions. Do not pick someone you feel you "relate" to closely; rather, choose someone whose experiences are different, someone who has another point of view. This will foster humility and spiritual growth for both or all of you.

The promises of serenity, freedom, and happiness always come true for those willing to work for them.

---

* The summary of the steps was adapted from *12 Steps to Loving Yourself* by Dorothy Marie England, ©1991 by Forward Movement, Cincinnati, Ohio. Used with permission.

About Forward Movement

Forward Movement inspires disciples and empowers evangelists. While we produce great resources like this book, Forward Movement is not a publishing company. We are a discipleship ministry. Publishing books, daily reflections, studies for small groups, and online resources are important ways we live out this ministry. People around the world read daily devotions through *Forward Day by Day*, which is also available in Spanish (*Adelante Dia a Dia*) and Braille, online, as a podcast, and as an app for your smartphone. We actively seek partners across the church and look for ways to provide resources that inspire and challenge. A ministry of the Episcopal Church since 1935, Forward Movement is a nonprofit organization funded by sales of resources and gifts from generous donors.

To learn more about Forward Movement and our work, visit us at forwardmovement.org or venadelante.org. We are delighted to be doing this work and invite your prayers and support.